Adventures in Blogging

Adventures in Blogging

Public Anthropology and Popular Media

Paul Stoller

UNIVERSITY OF TORONTO PRESS

Toronto Buffalo London

Library and Archives Canada Cataloguing in Publication

Stoller, Paul [Essays. Selections]
  Adventures in blogging : public anthropology and popular media / Paul Stoller.

Includes bibliographical references and index.
Issued in print and electronic formats.
ISBN 978-1-4875-9492-3 (softcover).—ISBN 978-1-4875-9493-0 (hardcover).—
ISBN 978-1-4875-9494-7 (EPUB).—ISBN 978-1-4875-9495-4 (PDF)

  1. Stoller, Paul—Blogs. 2. Blogs—Social aspects. 3. Blogs—Political aspects.
4. Online authorship. 5. Anthropology—Blogs. 6. Political science—Blogs.
7. Political sociology—Blogs. 8. Sociology—Blogs. I. Title.

HM851.S763 2018   302.23'14   C2017-905704-9
                                                                C2017-905705-7

We welcome comments and suggestions regarding any aspect of our publications—please feel free to contact us at news@utphighereducation.com or visit our Internet site at utorontopress.com.

North America
5201 Dufferin Street
North York, Ontario, Canada, M3H 5T8

2250 Military Road
Tonawanda, New York, USA, 14150

ORDERS PHONE: 1–800–565–9523
ORDERS FAX: 1–800–221–9985
ORDERS E-MAIL: utpbooks@utpress.utoronto.ca

UK, Ireland, and continental Europe
NBN International
Estover Road, Plymouth, PL6 7PY, UK
ORDERS PHONE: 44 (0) 1752 202301
ORDERS FAX: 44 (0) 1752 202333
ORDERS E-MAIL:
enquiries@nbninternational.com

Every effort has been made to contact copyright holders; in the event of an error or omission, please notify the publisher.

This book is printed on paper containing 100% post-consumer fibre.

The University of Toronto Press acknowledges the financial support for its publishing activities of the Government of Canada through the Canada Book Fund.

Printed in the United States of America.

Funded by the   Financé par le
Government   gouvernement
of Canada   du Canada   Canada

ALSO BY PAUL STOLLER

In Sorcery's Shadow (with Cheryl Olkes)
Fusion of the Worlds
The Taste of Ethnographic Things
The Cinematic Griot: The Ethnography of Jean Rouch
Embodying Colonial Memories
Sensuous Scholarship
Jaguar: A Story of Africans in America (a novel)
Money Has No Smell
Stranger in the Village of the Sick
Gallery Bundu (a novel)
The Power of the Between
Yaya's Story
Climbing the Mountain (with Mitchell Stoller)
The Sorcerer's Burden (a novel)

CONTENTS

PROLOGUE: BLOGGING BLISS AND PUBLIC ANTHROPOLOGY

From its beginnings, anthropology has had a significant public dimension. Franz Boas, the pioneer of American anthropology, was a very public figure, who in the early part of the 20th century protested against American racism and the interconnected toxins of eugenics and Social Darwinism. Almost 100 years later, these poisons have re-emerged strongly in the American and European public spheres. In a social and political context that celebrates ignorance and distrusts expertise, many people openly profess their belief that racial and ethnic minorities are inferior and that science is evil. A small group of these people has begun to engage in acts that are seemingly propelled by these beliefs—a spate of police killings of unarmed African American males, white nationalists attacking journalists, firebombing mosques, and killing innocent American citizens who happened to be African Americans (the Charleston church slaughter) or Muslims (a young teenage girl killed in Seattle). The re-emergence of these socially venomous conditions contributed to the perfect storm that led, in part, to the election of Donald J. Trump, a man who uses what Joseph Goebbels called "the big lie" to create a socially destructive "alternative reality."

There is a strong wind blowing in Europe and the United States, a wind that carries the dust of "the big lie." Here's the rub: no scholar—including, of course, anthropologists—can combat big lies with small truths. It's fine to practice anthropology as usual in order to better understand the emergence of global populism and its relation to globalization, international trade, worker migration, and technological change. In these troubled times, though, anthropologists can also use the eye-opening insights of ethnography to resist socially toxic big lies. Through blogs, editorials, accessible ethnographic texts, public appearances, performance, film, and art installations we can spread the anthropological word day after day, week after week, and year after year—a necessary and sufficient way for us to combat the celebration of ignorance and contribute to a more promising future. As scholars, is this not our central obligation?

An increasing number of anthropologists have taken up the challenge of public anthropology. There are any number of anthropological blogs, individual webpages, and social media platforms from which anthropologists, among other scholars, are attempting to critique climate change denial, racism, homophobia, gender discrimination, ethnic bias, income inequalities, health care inequities, and the culture of ignorance as well as the alternate reality of Trumpism. In her May 1, 2017 *Anthropology News* column, Alisse Waterston, then president of the American Anthropological Association, encouraged anthropology departments to consider more fully the academic value of public scholarship. She wrote:

> public anthropology includes such works as Roxanne Varzi's ethnographic novel *Last Scene Underground*; the spoken word, performance art, installation pieces, poetry and prose of Gina Athena Ulysse; Jason De León's powerful museum exhibit State of Exception/*Estado de Excepción*; Hugh Gusterson's columns in *Bulletin of the Atomic Scientists*; and an ever-growing number of anthropology blogs from Allegra Lab and Anthropology News to SAPIENS and Savage Minds. There's much more public scholarship I could name—but you get the idea.

All writers want a large and diverse audience to read their works. If only a few people are going to read what you produce, why toil and suffer all those long and lonely hours of screen staring, keyboard tapping, editing, re-editing, and sifting through readers' critical commentaries that require more screen staring, keyboard tapping, editing and re-editing? Is it enough, as I once thought, just to see your byline on a journal article or on a book's title page? In these techno-sophisticated times, how many colleagues, students, or—better yet—lay readers have the time or will to read seriously detailed, jargoned, and theorized anthropological writing about obscure groups of people living in remote parts of the world?

Having been in the anthropological game for a very long time, I find contemporary reading trends, which trouble me, poignantly evident. For most of my time in anthropology, I've been a book person. Sure, I wrote journal articles in the early years of my anthropological odyssey. I don't know if those "deadly competent" articles are better or worse than those of my contemporaries, but I do know that very few people have read them. When you ask someone about a journal article—even your journal article—see if the response is not something like "Oh, yes, I saw it," or "Right … I noticed it."

In our time-compressed era, people are less likely to say: "I've read your piece. Let's have some coffee to discuss it."

The same can be said for most anthropology books. Like most scholars, anthropologists tend to write books that will bring them a measure of disciplinary recognition. Given the constraining realities of academic institutions, most scholarly writers produce books that focus on here-and-now subjects for which they employ the most "sophisticated" theoretical frameworks. The result is that contemporary anthropological authors, for example, write works that meet the demands of institutional anthropology, which, in turn, set the stage for books of limited appeal. Such limited appeal makes publishers less than eager to publish anthropological works.

"We'll have to send it to marketing to see what they say."

Even anthropologists who use the reader-friendly elements of narrative, plot, sensuous evocation of place, and character development are finding it increasingly difficult to publish their books, let alone find a wide audience in an era of time-challenged readers. My own record of publication is a case in point. In more than 30 years of publishing narrative-style anthropological works, my first book, *In Sorcery's Shadow*, a memoir of my apprenticeship in Songhay sorcery, remains my most "successful" text. Since then, my sales figures have declined—even for subsequent memoirs that I, for one, consider more compelling works.

Is anyone out there reading our stuff?

BLOGGING BLISS

Because I wanted more people to read my writing, I decided to become a blogger. I started to blog on a research trip to Niger in 2009. After an absence of more than 18 years, I wanted to record my impressions of the countryside and the impact of cell phone technology on Nigerien social life. On the fifth anniversary of the death of the legendry Jean Rouch, I visited his gravesite in Niamey, Niger, and wrote a piece about his ethnographic and cinematic legacy. That blog triggered only a smattering of response. As I continued to blog, I slowly developed more of a following but also attracted an incredible torrent of parasitic Internet spammers. Given my sorry set of technological skills, I found it frustratingly time-consuming to manage the blog. Deciding to give up blogging, I posted my last personal blog on the eve of the 2010 congressional election. In that blog, I decried the celebration of ignorance in our political discourse.

Eventually, my friend and colleague Gina Ulysse, who had begun to blog at the *Huffington Post (HuffPost)*, convinced me to try my hand there (see Ulysse 2015). In December 2010 I posted my first *HuffPost* blog and have continued ever since. Since then I have been given the opportunity to present an anthropological spin on a wide variety of issues—American political discourse, electoral politics, tax policy, corporate culture, congressional deadlock, the celebration of (political) ignorance, foreign policy in West and North Africa, the social impact of technology, the return of Social Darwinism, the importance of the social contract, the impact of technology on education, and the politicization and corporatization of higher education. Having posted and read the responses to these blogs, I confess to having experienced blogging bliss: my anthropologically contoured ideas have been circulated broadly and widely. People far and wide whom I've never met and never will meet have responded—almost instantaneously—to what

I had written! Sometimes responders praise my essays. Sometimes they critique them rather caustically. Such immediate and spirited response, of course, is a sweet tonic for most writers whose deepest and most ongoing concern is that no one is paying attention to what they have produced.

BLOGGING BITES

As time has gone on, the intensity of my blogging bliss has diminished. There has been an uneven response to my *HuffPost* work. During the 2012 presidential primaries and general election, my anthropologically informed blogs on politics attracted intense, sometimes vitriolic responses. Following President Obama's reelection, my blogs on how ignorant politicians are waging war on the social sciences as well as blogs on the corporatization of public higher education had good distribution. The same can be said of my blogs on "The Anthropology of Trump." By contrast, my blogs on the cultural ramifications of the civil war in Mali or my essays on poverty in West Africa, which are topics that are woven into the fabric of my anthropological being, have sparked much less response—fewer comments, Facebook shares, or Twitter retweets.

If you write for a journalistic outfit like *HuffPost*, of course, your blog needs some sort of news hook that connects your particular material to a topic that is "in the news" of the moment. Given the rise of Trump in 2016–17, there has been much newsworthy material about which an anthropologist might blog. My blogs on "The Anthropology of Trump" have enjoyed wide circulation. But not all newsworthy blogs are about politics. In 2015, I wrote two blogs that defended ethnographic practices in the wake of the public controversy about Alice Goffman's bestselling ethnography, *On the Run*. Those blogs got quite a bit of play, as they say, in the blogosphere.

When you hit the right notes in a blog, your piece might be read by as many as 50,000 to 100,000 readers. In an *Anthrodendum* (formerly *Savage Minds*) interview (Anderson and Kendzior 2013), Sarah Kendzior, an anthropologist who regularly publishes pieces in a variety of high-circulation media outlets, said:

I recently wrote an article for *Al Jazeera*, "The Wrong Kind of Caucasian," that had a complicated premise but a simple conclusion: do not condemn people on the basis of their ethnic background or country of origin. It was read by half a million people and shared on Facebook 57,000 times. I got letters from people saying I had changed their preconceptions and that they were going to keep an open mind about race, ethnicity, and immigration. It felt good to make a difference in a politically heated time.

In this case of blogosphere bliss, blogging is anthropological expression that has public impact. And yet, there are limitations to blogging for outlets like *HuffPost*, the *Washington Post*, or *Psychology Today*. There is some degree of topical limitation—the aforementioned news angle. There is also the bane of all journalistic writing/blogging: space limitation. Outlets like *HuffPost* prefer to publish essays that are short and snappy—850 words or less. They assume that anything longer will challenge the limited attention spans of fickle readers who like to site surf on the Internet. Given the limitations of space, it is quite difficult to advance a nuanced argument or confront the complexity of a social issue. There is also the question of duration. If you're lucky, a *HuffPost* blog will be "live" for 24 to 36 hours. If you're really lucky, an editor will decide to "promote" your blog, maybe even to the Front Page, which sometimes extends the blog's shelf life. Even the most popular, favorited, and trending blogs quickly fade away to make room for the next hour's or next day's collection of blogs that will in their turn be promoted, trending, and popular.

So, if you're an anthropologist who blogs on a public platform like *HuffPost*, you can attract a huge audience that will most likely be exposed to only a sliver of your knowledge.

Is the sacrifice worth it?

I think it is.

Any anthropologically informed contribution to public discourse promotes the public good. Even so, I don't think that the attraction of anthropological blogging and other forms of public anthropology should compel us to abandon our quest to understand more fully the human condition or our desire to comprehend the dimensions of human well-being. These complicated and multifaceted issues are at the very center of anthropological thought and practice and do not always lend themselves to the space limitations and the nanosecond half-lives you find in the blogosphere.

Is there a happy medium?

Several observers like Patrick Dunleavy are not particularly worried about the declining prestige of paper books and articles in the academy. In a 2013 essay in the *LSE Review of Books*, he sees the diminished importance of books from a technological vantage. Dunleavy suggests that paper books and journals are outmoded. As long as "book-loving" academics are in what he calls "digital denial," the number of people inclined to read what social scientists write will continue to dwindle. Moving to more digital representations of social science works, he suggests, will result in greater textual distribution, lower priced e-books, and free open access journal articles. Put another way, Dunleavy argues that digital formats will eventually bring back the prestige of academic books and essays.

Dunleavy overlooks an important factor: the accessibility of content. A digital format cannot guarantee that a wide audience of readers will consume social science writing—especially if scholars continue to write their works in turgid, jargon-laden prose. Even in digital formats, bad writing disconnects readers from writers. No matter the format, works that remain open to the world are usually those in which writers use narratives—stories—to connect with their readers. Those are the texts that endure, texts that people may well be reading 10, 20, or even 50 years after their initial publication. As the great American novelist Tim O'Brien wrote in his incomparable novel, *The Things They Carried*: "Stories are for those late hours in the night when you can't remember how you got from where you were to where you are. Stories are for an eternity, when memory is erased, when there is nothing to remember except for the story" (1990: 38).

The digital revolution alone will not make us better storytelling scholars who are able to connect meaningfully to a wide audience of digitally connected readers. If my experience is indicative, the most important ramification of public blogging is that it makes you a better writer. Blogging, I think, has made my academic writing snappier, more concise, and more focused on the connections I want to make with readers. Like any writer, I want to produce work—no matter the technological format—that may move some readers to think new thoughts, make new connections, or even feel new feelings. If I can sometimes produce work that realizes that goal, I am meeting my fundamental obligation as a scholar: to produce knowledge that makes life a little bit sweeter.

In *Adventures in Blogging,* I attempt to show how blogging can bring an important anthropological perspective to public debate. This book is not a set of prescriptions on anthropological blogging; rather, it presents blogs that I wrote in reaction to public events from 2011 to 2017. As such, the blogs here presented show how a new generation of anthropologists can bring their increasingly important anthropological perspective to contemporary political debate—"The Anthropology of Trump," for example. The blogs in this book also show how anthropological bloggers can reveal the hidden dynamics of political power and the increasing need for public social science. By the same token, the chapters in *Adventures in Blogging* also demonstrate how public blogging can help to shape higher education policy and practice—a critique of the corporatization and bureaucratization of the university. The anthropologically informed blogs presented in this book also showcase how expert testimony can add flesh and bones to thin media representations of world events, especially those emanating from the Middle East and Africa. Finally, there are blogs in *Adventures in Blogging* that underscore fundamentally existential matters: the drama of health and illness in everyday life as well as explorations of the cultural dimensions of human well-being. How do we cope with chronic illness in our quest for well-being?

The practices of anthropology are time-honored. Anthropologists have long conducted fieldwork throughout the world. This intensive and personal research intervention has produced the ethnographic record—a highly detailed and nuanced inventory of books and films that describe with finesse the social lives of peoples far and near. That inventory, in turn, has compelled anthropologists to reflect upon the whys and wherefores of the human condition, a set of ideas about how human beings live in the world. It is, in short, an enviable record of scholarship. Despite this enviable record, anthropological writing has had a narrow reach in a digitally interconnected world in which modern citizens increasingly extract their knowledge from the Internet. If we are to remain viable scholars, future anthropologists will need to represent their knowledge in forms in addition to the long-standing genre of the academic monograph. This book is an attempt to demonstrate the utility of alternate communication technologies—blogging, in this case—to communicate culture in the 21st century.

Adventures in Blogging is divided into five sections, all of which showcase the power of blogs to communicate anthropological insights to the public. In Part One, "Blogging Politics in the Age of Trump," the blogs demonstrate how an engaged political anthropology can help to pave the way for a sustained resistance to the authoritarian politics of Donald Trump. They also demonstrate how the increasing importance of celebrity culture in America set the stage for a politics of dysfunction that feeds upon conspiracy theories. These "theories" have constructed a parallel reality based upon a discourse of "alternative facts." Part Two, "Blogging Social Science," features blogs that show the power of social science to reveal unseen dimensions in society, dimensions that can determine the fate of public politics or the results of local, regional, or national elections. The corporatization of the university is the focus of the blogs in Part Three, "Blogging Higher Education: A Public Defense of Scholarship." In various ways, these blogs demonstrate how business models lead to bloated university bureaucracies and unproductive "make-work," which, in turn, weaken the vital bond between professor and student. The final two parts of the book are "Blogging Media" (Part Four) and "Blogging and Well-Being" (Part Five). The blogs in these sections are less political than those in previous parts of the book. The entries on media demonstrate why anthropological expertise, especially in non-European parts of the world, is needed to understand the social complexity of our globally integrated world. In Part Four I attempt to show how more anthropologically contoured blogs on social, economic, and political life in Africa can lead to increased public comprehension of global complexities. Blogging can also help us to understand fundamental existential issues linked to health and illness and death and dying, as illustrated in Part Five. The themes articulated in these blogs can sometimes bring anthropologically contoured comfort to readers who are suffering from chronic illnesses or from cultural alienation. In the Epilogue, "Anthropology and Popular Media," I return to a more general discussion of public anthropology and suggest how public writing and representation might be integrated into the training of future scholars. If scholars can produce good stories that connect with broadly based audiences, we have much to contribute to debate in the public sphere.

As the chapters in *Adventures in Blogging* suggest, public anthropologists are wonderfully positioned—experientially, intellectually, and technologically—to contribute significantly to the future play of policy, social movements, and politics. We have the wherewithal to use our knowledge to make life more comprehensible, which, in turn, improves our being-in-world.

PART ONE

BLOGGING POLITICS IN THE AGE OF TRUMP

INTRODUCTION

These days just about everyone engages in some form of blogging. If you post a message on Facebook, or make a comment about something that you have retweeted, you are microblogging. If you post a photo with a caption on Instagram, you are also microblogging. These messages, which can be terse or detailed, can be about a wide variety of subjects. These may be personal (family relations, birthdays, reunions, travel, medical updates), social (comments about race relations, income and/or health inequities, grassroots social movements), professional (notification of conferences, announcements of grant awards and article and book publications), or political (commentary on public policy, the effectiveness of government, or a political campaign). No matter the subject, a personal microblog is an invitation for an online conversation, which is, in turn, an invitation to connect or reconnect with people in a digital network.

The public blogs that constitute *Adventures in Blogging* differ from personal posts. Like personal posts, public blogs are invitations to a conversation. Indeed, if a public blog is widely shared on Facebook or retweeted on Twitter, it prompts both online and off-line conversations. The public blog, however, is longer and more detailed than a microblog. The goal of the public blog, moreover, is to reach readers

I

beyond the blogger's personal network. In addition, the public blog usually showcases some degree of expertise about a wide assortment of subjects. If the expertise is communicated in a short, plainly articulated text, it may attract a large and diverse audience. For scholars, the public blog is one way to communicate insights, derived through rigorous research and scholarly reflection, to an increasingly wired-in audience. Blogging, then, is an effective way to contribute slowly developed insights in a culture of speed and expedience.

In this part of *Adventures in Blogging*, I present public political blogs that I wrote for the *Huffington Post* in quick response to a variety of political events. My take on contemporary politics, however, is based on years of slowly cultivated thinking about politics in social life. In most of the posts, which are succinct texts comprising short paragraphs, I try to make one point in clear and compelling prose. In some of the blogs, I use narrative techniques—description and dialogue. The political blog is therefore a relatively slow intervention in the culture of speed.

Politics provides a wonderful domain for anthropological reflection. In the United States, politics has become a profoundly social and cultural arena of public debate. Considering that much of the political commentary on television and radio often amounts to—at best—fast and shallow reflection, it is incumbent on anthropologists, among other scholars, to join the conversation. Given the long record of anthropological thinking about social relations and cultural concepts, anthropologists are particularly well placed to write about the practice of politics-in-the-world.

Classic and more recent anthropological concepts can be powerfully employed to explain the behaviors of politicians like Israeli Prime Minister Bibi Netanyahu, President Barack Obama, Florida Governor Rick Scott, or more recently President Donald J. Trump. Anthropological concepts can be used to understand how political institutions like the US Congress function in the turbulent climate of extreme partisanship. They can be employed to probe the social and cultural ramifications of laws like the Affordable Care Act and to consider the social consequences of Republican efforts to replace Obamacare with Trumpcare. Anthropological bloggers are well situated to shed light on the social impact of policies that affect our fragile environment. They can also use their blogs to resist political oppression and the power of "the big lie."

In academic writing, we tend to tell our readers about things. We articulate a complex argument that refines our thinking about culture, social relations, the evolutionary record, or the dynamics of politics. Indeed, I could go on and on about how an anthropological perspective brings depth and breadth to ongoing political debate.

In our digitally interconnected world, though, blogging politics on wide-circulation social media news platforms like *HuffPost*, *Slate*, and *Salon* can be a central element in the practice of contemporary public anthropology. These platforms require timely essays that are short, crisp, and accessible to the general public. When a political event occurs, the anthropologically informed political blogger who follows the news regularly decides which item she or he can write about with a degree of expertise and then responds with dispatch. The news landscape, after all, is ever-shifting.

How do you link news material to anthropological concepts? In the political blogs that follow, I've tried to produce such linkages. In March 2016, when candidate Donald Trump swept the Super Tuesday Republican primaries to assure his presidential nomination, I posted on *HuffPost* "The Anthropology of Trump" (see Chapter 7), in which I tried to demonstrate how the American culture of celebrity had, in large measure, propelled his victories.

The relatively speedy practice of blogging in the popular media may seem like an affront to the slow work of anthropology in which scholars spend years engaged in study, reflection, and writing to produce faithful representations of social life. That pursuit is a noble one. Public political blogs, however, are not an affront to established anthropological practice, for bloggers can—and do—employ slowly developed anthropological concepts. In the political blogs that follow, I use such time-honored concepts as economic exchange, social class, culture, and race to craft my posts. These deliberately developed concepts can be used to compose hard-hitting political blogs that make one powerful point in 850 clearly and simply expressed words. It sounds daunting, but with practice, it can be done with great efficacy—a very good way to engage in the public anthropology of contemporary American politics.

CHAPTER ONE

POLITICS IN A CULTURE OF IGNORANCE

(MARCH 2011)

During the past few weeks, the play of American politics has been particularly disturbing. Consider the willful ignorance of former Arkansas Governor Mike Huckabee, trying to convince his supporters that President Obama is "not one of us." To that end, he suggested that President Obama's worldview was shaped by his childhood in Kenya—or maybe it was Indonesia—and by radical movements like the Kenyan Mau-Mau revolt. Huckabee, a potential Republican candidate for president, went on to say that President Obama's father and grandfather molded his "foreign" ideas about how the world works. It doesn't matter that President Obama hardly knew his father or his paternal grandfather, or that the Mau-Mau rebellion took place far from the Obama homestead in Kenya, a country President Obama first visited when he was 26 years old. Governor Huckabee also failed to mention the "inconvenient truths" that President Obama was raised by his mother and his maternal grandparents who grew up in Kansas or that President Obama's maternal grandfather fought with Patton in Europe during World War II.

Think about the countless numbers of elected officials, Republicans all, who say that "we" are "broke," a rather bombastic overstatement, because of greedy public employees. Due to the "lazy" greed of these middle-income public servants, the argument goes, we need to abolish collective bargaining and eviscerate budgets for education, the arts, the environment, and even law enforcement. What else can you do when it is a sin to either raise taxes or scale back corporate tax breaks? What's more, there is no room for negotiation on these matters, which means that there is no space for conceptual nuance, and little or no willingness for a civil exchange of ideas that might result in compromise—the foundation of the American political system.

Looking at these developments from a more or less rational standpoint, none of it makes much sense. How can any reasonably intelligent person, you might ask yourself, accept the big lie that many conservative Republicans have long touted: that the simple formula of lower taxes and limited government will somehow solve all of the complex economic and social problems in a globally integrated world? And yet that is the pabulum that a whole host of Republican presidential hopefuls offer again and again to their base and, through media coverage, to the rest of us. If you repeat the big lie often enough, some people—many people, in fact—begin to believe it.

Are contemporary American politics being played out in a culture of ignorance? What does it say about contemporary political culture when there is political support for uncompromising public figures who seem more interested in unrealistic ideological purity than governing their polities? How else can you explain the political support and media attention we give to politicians like Sarah Palin or Michele Bachmann or Mike Huckabee? Even though they unflaggingly demonstrate an acute intellectual incompetence as well as wholesale ignorance of American history and world affairs, they still manage to maintain or even increase their legions of followers. Is there no political price to pay for incompetence or ignorance?

It is no easy task to try to explain this descent into a culture of ignorance. Some of the descent may be rooted in our underfunded and unfairly maligned system of public education. As a professor at a public university I have firsthand knowledge of the processes that give rise to a culture of ignorance. Although the intelligence, curiosity, and grit of some of my students, many of whom are the first people in their families to attend college, thoroughly inspires me, I am often shocked and disappointed by general student ignorance of culture, geography, history, and politics—at home and abroad. Even more disturbing is what seems to be a lack of student curiosity about a world that has been rendered more complex through globalization. Many of my students are not interested in learning about foreign societies. They take my introductory cultural anthropology course because it is a requirement. In addition, some of my students seek the most expedient path toward graduation—one that involves the least amount of work and difficulty for the greatest return. The upshot is that many students leave the university unprepared to compete in the global economy. Many of them have trouble thinking critically. Others find doing any kind of research to be profoundly challenging. Some write essays that border on the incoherent. More troubling still is that this downward spiral toward incompetence, according to the findings of Richard Arum and Josipa Roksa's new book, *Academically Adrift: Limited Learning on College Campuses*, seems to be widespread among our college and university students.

If this picture reflects the intellectual state of our college students, what can we say about the capacity of the general public to critically evaluate a complex set of information? The only way to reverse this slide into mediocrity, which is reflected in both the intellectual quality of contemporary politics and the distressing climate of our educational institutions, is to make serious investments in education and the public sector in order to give to our underpaid and underappreciated teachers and civil servants the support and respect they deserve. To do otherwise is to risk sinking even deeper into the swamp.

CHAPTER TWO

ANTI-ANTI SCIENCE

(MARCH 2011)

It's getting crazy out there in the land of politics. At a recent Republican forum in Iowa, representatives Ron Paul and Michele Bachmann spoke of the wonders of home schooling. In so doing, Paul characterized public education as "indoctrination." This claim suggests that public school teachers are brainwashing our children and grandchildren. If Representative Bachmann's recent public demonstration of historical knowledge, or her long-standing incapacity to articulate a coherently logical argument, is representative of home-school teaching, then home schooling needs a great deal of retooling. Indeed, if her demonstrated knowledge and intellect reflect the "strengths" of home schooling, how will home-schooled kids be able to compete in the world, let alone be capable of creative or critical thinking, which is, lest we forget, the foundation of any viable democracy?

The claim of public school "indoctrination" is part and parcel of a powerful wave of anti-science rhetoric that has been promoted in recent American political discourse. There is, for example, much suspicion of climate science, which many right-wing ideologues consider a bogus pursuit of knowledge. In February of last year, the Utah legislature passed a bill that disputes the science of climate change, arguing that greenhouse emissions are "essentially harmless." In that bill as reported by Suzanne Goldenberg in the *Guardian*, the Utah legislature, claiming that global warming is a hoax, demands that the Environmental Protection Agency (EPA) halt its attempts to regulate greenhouse gases. Speaking of such regulation, Utah Representative Mike Noel said: "Sometimes ... we need the courage to do nothing."

Anti-science thinking has worked its way into the Republican Caucus of the US House of Representatives. On February 19 of this year, the House voted 244 to 179 to kill the US funding of the Intergovernmental Panel on Climate Change (IPCC). Although this nonpartisan organization won a Nobel Prize in 2007 for its sobering array of climate change assessments, the majority in the House sided with Representative Blaine Luetkemeyer (R) of Missouri who referred to IPCC scientists as "nefarious" practitioners whose "corrupt" findings are part of an alarmist conspiracy. House Republicans believed so strongly in Representative Leutkemeyer's set of anti-science assumptions that they ignored the report of the Department of Commerce's inspector general who, after an examination of the leaked emails of several climate scientists—the source for claims of "corrupt" findings—found no evidence of wrongdoing or, for that matter, "nefarious" science.

The congressional anti-science crusade shows no sign of slowing down. On March 3 of this year Representative Fred Upton (R) of Michigan and Senator James Inhofe (R) of Oklahoma introduced legislation that may well pass in the House of Representatives, that strips the Environmental Protection Agency (EPA) of the power to regulate carbon dioxide emissions. Against overwhelming and long-standing scientific evidence, they argue that carbon pollution poses no threat to public health and the environment.

How can we account for what from a rational perspective seems like anti-science lunacy? How can 244 members of the House of Representatives vote to deny US funding to the IPCC, which won the Nobel Prize in 2007? From my anthropological vantage, it seems that a vibrant anti-science culture is emerging in the US. Deeply rooted in fundamentalist religious beliefs, the culture of anti-science is creating an alternative universe of meaning in which scientific practices and findings, which tend to subvert fundamentalist social and cultural and political principles, are suspect and/or dismissed.

In the culture of science, there is open-ended critical debate. As new data are generated, they are critically scrutinized. This ongoing method means that scientists and social scientists are continuously assessing their practices and testing their ideas for reliability and validity, which, in turn, means that methods, ideas, and theories are always being altered and refined. This set of scientific practices has advanced knowledge immeasurably. In short, the culture of science has provided a conceptual and practical framework that has enabled an exponential increase in the quality of our lives in the world.

The culture of anti-science, by contrast, has a narrow focus. In such a culture, beliefs about the world are often based on selective attention to scientific information or, worse yet, conspiracy theories. In this culture, one's belief tends to be ironclad. Even if an organization like the highly esteemed IPCC or the EPA presents an overwhelming case for, say, climate change or the negative impact of carbon emissions on public health and the environment, people who are anti-science will not be impressed. They will not change their minds or their positions. For them, the "common sense" of the culture of anti-science trumps the long-standing and critically productive methods of the culture of science. When 244 Republicans in the House of Representatives vote to cut US IPCC funding, they are suggesting that they somehow have the inside track to the truth of things, that they know what is good for public health and the environment. Such a vote, I'm afraid, is a sad and unfortunate institutional celebration of ignorance.

As a social scientist who studies the concept of culture, global social transformations, and the ever-changing practices of religion, I am anti anti-science, which means that I feel obliged to comment critically on the ideas and practices of my own academic discipline, but steadfastly defend the culture of science, a culture that enables such a critical discourse. Like all scientists, I am against close-minded conspiratorial thinking that allows little or no dissent, a thinking that in its celebration of ignorance looks backward into the darkness.

Although the elected officials who are proponents of the culture of anti-science sometimes make statements that appear either comedic or idiotic to any reasonable person, they are promoting ideas that endanger the future of our children and grandchildren. To secure our future, we need to make sure that the unschooled—possibly home schooled—advocates of the culture of anti-science articulate their ideas far from the halls of government where such advocacy undermines the public good.

CHAPTER THREE

CLASS ILLUSIONS

There's been a great deal of talk about social class in recent political discourse. Whenever President Obama says he wants to tax the rich, Republican politicians say he is engaging in "class warfare." Democrats strike back, saying that class battles have been going on for a very long time and that, in fact, the rich have pretty much won the war. They then worry about the erosion of the middle class, which corresponds to the ever-expanding gap between haves and have-nots and the increasing number of our fellow citizens living in poverty.

Like the notion of race, social class is a multifaceted, hard-to-define concept. It's a subject we don't like to talk about in America.

When I teach introductory anthropology classes I always ask my students how many of them are middle class.

Everyone in the classroom raises his or her hand. In more than 30 years of teaching these courses, no one has ever volunteered that they are "working class" or "lower class." By the same token, no one has said they are "upper class." When I ask the students how they determine a person's social class, they invariably suggest that it depends upon income, education, and occupation. But they can never agree what income level makes you middle class as opposed to working class, lower middle class, upper middle class, or upper class.

There is similar disagreement about occupation and education. Can we include in the middle class a public school teacher with a graduate degree who makes a paltry $40,000 a year? Can we include in the upper middle class a master plumber with no university degree, who earns $300,000 a year?

The teacher has a low salary, but knows a great deal about art. Does knowledge of the arts make you middle class, upper middle class, or upper class?

The plumber has a large house and a swimming pool, but knows little about literature. Can such a lack of classical knowledge exclude him from the upper middle class?

And what about the earthy Texas oilman who has donated millions of dollars to museums and universities? Do these donations make him an American patrician?

And what about the "old money" patrician who has lost his family's fortune? Does his knowledge of yachts, polo, and debutante balls make him upper class?

If you look beneath the surface of social class, it is clear that it's difficult to define it through objective criteria. Our perception of social class tends to be subjective and deeply embedded in our culture. Like race, it is a concept that uses perceived social and economic status to divide Americans into distinct groups.

And yet, we try our best to avoid thinking about class division in America. Like my students, most Americans want to believe that they are middle class, and this notion, which goes along with the myths of American social equality and equal opportunity, makes us feel good. We don't like to discuss issues that threaten our social myths, the stories we like to tell ourselves about ourselves.

In the game of power, however, those who want to maintain their authority and legitimacy spin myths that make "the people" feel good about themselves. In so doing they create smokescreens that obscure what's really going on. In the current debate about President Obama's proposed jobs bill, Republicans cynically cry "class warfare." They don't want us to ponder the inconvenient fact that the middle class is eroding, that almost 50 million of our fellow citizens do not have health insurance, or that the gap between rich and poor has now expanded to record levels. They cry "class warfare" to convince us that the "evil" government wants to take your hard-earned money and give it to some unemployed person too lazy to look for a job. They cry "class warfare" to hide a redistribution of wealth that takes the hard-earned money of working Americans and gives it to the rich— maintaining corporate tax loopholes, granting rebates to oil companies, and extending the Bush tax cuts.

It is perhaps a sad truth, but it seems that most Republicans have come to believe that telling the "Big Lie" works well in the arena of politics. Contrary to the historical record, they say again and again that you can reduce the deficit, to take one of many examples, by lowering taxes. Even though this doesn't make any mathematical sense, they repeat this mantra again and again, convincing millions of "middle class" and "working class" people to vote *against* their interests.

It's time for Democrats and Independents to begin to employ the Big Truth. As inconvenient as these truths might be, if we repeat the mantras again and again we may be able to convince millions of "middle class" and "working class" people to vote *for* their interests and reaffirm the American social contract.

CHAPTER FOUR

SOCIAL ENGINEERING AND THE POLITICS OF IGNORANCE

(JULY 2012)

One of my Facebook friends is a wonderful guy who sometimes lambasts my public criticism of trends in American society. Most recently, he didn't like the fact that I thought that the trains in Germany, which I rode in April, were fast, clean, and on time, whereas the trains in the US, which I take regularly, are slow, dirty, and late. He wondered if I ever had anything good to say about America. In another exchange, he called President Obama a communist.

I asked my friend, whom I like and respect, if he had taken a train lately.

No response.

I also pointed out to him that Marx's writings were mostly about how societies change (and not by communist revolution) and that there has never been a truly "communist" society. I suggested that it's really hard to find communists these days, unless you go to France or Italy, and even there they are few and far between.

No response.

My friend, in short, had little if any empirical evidence for his statements. He may have read Marx, but didn't say so. He may have taken a train, but remained silent on that matter.

Like millions of Americans these days, he might have "heard" that President Obama is a communist. In the same vein, he, like millions of Americans, might have "heard" that Barack Obama is a Muslim who was born in Kenya. Contrary to overwhelming evidence, most of the folks who have "heard" about these things have an unyielding belief that they are true.

There are other wacky beliefs that have slipped into the American imaginary.

- In Louisiana children are being taught that the so-called "presence" of the Loch Ness monster, which only seems to appear if you've consumed the entire contents of a particularly powerful bottle of Single Malt Scotch, proves that dinosaurs co-exist with humans. Contrary to more than 100 years of rigorous science that upholds Darwin's ideas, the "Nessy" evidence suggests that evolutionary theory is not "settled."
- In Texas, the GOP platform has come out against "critical thinking skills," suggesting that such thinking subverts traditional values. Here's the text from the platform document.

> We oppose the teaching of Higher Order Thinking Skills (HOTS) (values clarification), critical thinking skills and similar programs that are simply a relabeling of Outcome-Based Education (OBE) (mastery learning) which focus on behavior modification and have the purpose of challenging the student's fixed beliefs and undermining parental authority.

Backtracking, a bit, the Texas GOP said that this carefully phrased part of the platform was a "mistake," which is hard to believe. Even so, it remains part of the official Texas GOP platform.

- In Tennessee, Governor Bill Haslam allowed a bill to become law that allows the teaching of creationism in the state's classrooms.

How can so many people be so arrogantly ignorant?

From my vantage as an educator and an anthropologist, I'd say there are two interrelated factors that account for this sobering phenomenon: a widespread and sharp decline in reading and thinking capacities; and an attempt to return to the Gilded Age through what Newt Gingrich, of all people, called "social engineering."

The data on American reading and thinking patterns are disturbing.

Based on investigative journalist Brian Ross's reporting, here's a sample of the findings of a broad survey on American Adult Literacy conducted by the National Center for Education Statistics.

- 21–23% of adult Americans demonstrated the lowest level of skills, performing simple, routine tasks involving brief and uncomplicated texts and documents. They could total an entry on a deposit slip, locate the time or place of a meeting on a form, and identify a piece of specific information in a brief news article. Many in this level of the survey were unable to perform most or all of the tasks, and some had such limited skills that they were unable to respond to much of the survey.
- 25–28% of adult Americans demonstrated skills in the next higher level of proficiency (Level 2) although their ability to grasp complex information was still quite limited. They were generally able to locate information in text, to make low-level inferences using printed materials, and to integrate easily identifiable pieces of information.
- The approximately 90 million American adults who performed in Levels 1 and 2 did not necessarily perceive themselves as being nearly functionally illiterate.

Mr. Ross's conclusions are eye-opening. Among American adults, a mere 20% have the capacity to understand the nuances of politics and public policy. More than half the population of American adults cannot make sense of the complex information patterns that shape public policy. These findings may not matter, because, as Mr. Ross states, most Americans get their information "from TV, or conversations with friends and co-workers." They "hear" things and consider those things to be true.

Given the impoverished state of American literacy, is it any wonder that negative political ads, so filled with half-truths, misleading statements, and boldface lies, have had such an impact on millions of adults who vote for propositions and candidates whose ideas and agendas are bound to make their lives more difficult, if not painful.

Enter the second factor—the attempt to return American society to the extreme social inequality and social divisions of the Gilded Age, in which everyone knew his or her place. If you have a viable middle class, such a return is impossible. And so the GOP, which indirectly advocates such a position, has been promoting policies (slashing education funding, opposing critical thinking skills, undermining labor unions, cutting social services) that shrink the middle class and make it more and more difficult to achieve the American Dream. The GOP has garnered support for these policies and the politicians who promote them by spending lavishly on aforementioned negative political ads. Such advertising convinces struggling people to be against health care initiatives that would improve their lives; it compels them to vote for candidates whose agendas would undermine their social well-being. Propaganda works best when its audience is uninformed.

If we allow the politics of ignorance to solidify its hold on the political imagination, we condemn ourselves to a dark future. If we get all the news we need from the weather report, as Simon and Garfunkel say in their remarkably prophetic song, there will be many stormy days ahead.

CHAPTER FIVE

RACING AWAY FROM FERGUSON AND THE CHALLENGE OF EDUCATION

(DECEMBER 2014)

As the holidays approach, we are racing toward a point of social upheaval in America. The killings of Michael Brown in Ferguson, Missouri, and Eric Garner in New York City have brought into bright relief the utter ugliness of police behavior toward young African American men in our cities and small towns. That behavior has resulted in the unnecessary deaths of young men who for the most part were in the wrong place at the wrong time. That behavior demonstrates the centrality of race and racism in contemporary American social life.

Although my fellow anthropologists routinely discuss with good measures of lucidity the issue of race in American society, it is not a subject that most mainstream Americans want to discuss. Anthropologists have demonstrated powerfully that race is unquestionably a social construct that is used to maintain our ever-increasing system of social inequality—an inequality that is economic, political, and most importantly judicial. As a society, we are racing away from Ferguson. The specter of racism makes us want to avoid the discomfort of talking about how race is a central structure in the foundation of contemporary American society.

Think about our society. We suffer from a growing system of economic inequality. There is an unequal access to wealth, to education, to health services, to good food, to peaceful parks and centers of recreation. There is also the digital divide. How many people do you know who can't afford a computer or Internet access? How many people do you know who wait in line to use a computer at the public library? How many people do you know who take inadequate public transportation like the local bus or the Greyhound?

As a society we ignore poverty and racism because it undermines our fundamental America myths. Ferguson tells us that America is neither the land of equal opportunity nor a place that has freed itself from prejudice. The police killings in Ferguson and Cleveland and New York City tell us that hate, blind ignorance, and brutal violence present "clear and present" dangers to our society.

What can be done?

Protests may shed light on racial and ethnic discrimination, but they won't eradicate a problem that is fundamentally social and cultural. Political action has sometimes shed light on the problem, but profoundly silent attitudes about racial and/or ethnic prejudice, which are part and parcel of our cultural system, will take a long time to change.

My own sense is that the battle for change, for reconstructing the social contract, for social justice and for human dignity, must be waged in our classrooms and on our college campuses. Although we like to say that much progress toward social justice has been made in America, there are signs that a surprising percentage of our students, who will soon direct our civic life, are filled with levels of ignorance and hate that will challenge educators for many years to come. Consider a recent letter from the Faculty Senate at my university about student reaction to an ongoing peaceful "Black Lives Matter" demonstration on our campus.

> Demonstrations were organized and held on campus Friday and again today by students who were protesting recent judicial rulings. The rallies were powerful and peaceful and addressed the issues of police response, race and racism. Students who organized these protests were committed to their message and used known peaceful strategies of social change to get their points heard.

Sadly, the reactions by some students to the protests were extremely concerning. Demonstrators heard vile and racist comments said by people walking past. On social media students also posted vile and racist comments about the demonstrations and the participants.

If such vile hate is easily found at my university, which has a typically diverse student body, you have to wonder about the level of hate in environments less dedicated, to quote our university president in a Dec. 8 letter to the campus community, to "the exchange of ideas through civil dialogue."

The issues of race and racism have long been part and parcel of American culture. What will become of them in the 21st century when America becomes less white and more ethnically and culturally diverse? In my cultural anthropology classes I suggest that there are two paths to the social future. The first path is the well-worn trail of hate, discrimination, and economic apartheid. Those who follow that path want to take us back to a future of cultural homogeneity. The second path is one of inclusivity. Those who choose that path will attempt to weave our ever-increasing diversity into the social fabric.

Ecologists suggest that systems that incorporate difference remain adaptable and robust. By the same token, those systems that destroy difference become less and less resistant to change and eventually fade away. If you destroy that which is different, following the sage analysis of A. David Napier in his path-breaking book, *The Age of Immunology*, you eventually weaken your system as it becomes a paler and paler imitation of itself. When we reject otherness, Napier reminds us, do we not we reject ourselves? Is not the attachment and growth of the human embryo the most fundamental inclusion of difference and otherness that we know? Indeed, such inclusion ensures the viability of our species.

Our challenge in the Anthropocene, then, is a fundamentally anthropological one—to design courses of instruction in which these ecological, social, and cultural truths are clearly articulated. In this way our students will be able to make an informed choice about which future path they want to follow.

The times are perilous. We are confronting a potentially devastating set of ecological, social, and cultural crises, which means that as scholars we have a great obligation. It's time for us to step up to the plate.

CHAPTER SIX

BIG MAN BIBI

(MARCH 2015)

The prospect of Israeli Prime Minister Benjamin "Bibi" Netanyahu's speech to a joint session of the US Congress has generated a great deal of political heat. People in the Obama administration have been outraged that a foreign leader is coming to America two weeks before his own hotly contested bid for reelection to critique American foreign policy toward Iran. This action not only ignores diplomatic protocol but undermines President Obama.

Indeed, Prime Minister Netanyahu has made no secret of his appreciation for the Republicans in Congress, politicians who routinely insult President Obama. Led by Speaker of the House John Boehner, the House Republicans unilaterally orchestrated the prime minister's invitation to address the US Congress. As many commentators have pointed out, such an invitation—and the prime minister's acceptance of it—is a provocation designed to undercut delicate ongoing nuclear negotiations between Iran and the US, negotiations that are creeping toward resolution. In the absence of such an agreement, it is equally clear that Prime Minister Netanyahu and many of his Republican friends in the US Congress think that military action is the best way to resolve the issue of Iranian nuclear capacities.

The political firestorm that Prime Minister Netanyahu's visit has provoked has not deterred Bibi. He is resolute in his belief that Iran, which he has called a suicide state, intends to build and use nuclear weapons to destroy the Jewish state. When he discusses these issues, he wears a very special cloak that envelopes him in a new messianic identity: the Protector of the Jews.

The Protector will not be stopped.

The Protector says he knows what's best for Jews like me. He knows what's best for the world. It doesn't matter to him that Meir Dagan, the former director of the Mossad, has stated that Bibi has exaggerated the dangers of Iran's nuclear program. Memos leaked from Israeli intelligence sources suggest that nuclear production activities in Iran are not consistent with a program of weapons development.

The Protector will not be stopped.

It doesn't matter to Bibi that the director of the American Anti-Defamation League, Abraham Foxman, a leading voice in the American Jewish community, urged him to cancel his trip.

As reported in the *Huffington Post* on February 7:

> Abraham Foxman ... a leading voice in the Jewish community, told The Jewish Daily Forward that the controversy over Netanyahu's speech is unhelpful. He added that Netanyahu should stay home.
>
> "One needs to restart, and it needs a mature adult statement that this was not what we intended," Foxman said in an interview published Friday. "It has been hijacked by politics. Now is a time to recalibrate...."

The Protector will not be stopped.

It doesn't matter to him that a *Wall Street Journal*/NBC News poll published on March 1 reported that roughly half of US registered voters disapprove of John Boehner's decision to invite Netanyahu to speak without asking President Barack Obama.

In the face of such powerful opposition, how can we account for Bibi's stubborn determination? Why is he so resolute? Why all the bluster and bombast?

Anthropologists have a deceptively simple answer: Bibi is behaving like a Melanesian Big Man. In New Guinea societies, men who seek prestige in the social arena—usually the men's ceremonial house—used bluster and bombast to gain personal advantage and prestige. In his classic work *Naven*, Gregory Bateson, one of the great thinkers of the 20th century, described this exaggerated and bombastic behavior among New Guinea's Iatmul people:

> An important man on entering the ceremonial house is conscious that the public eye is upon him and he responds to this stimulus with some sort of over-emphasis. He will enter with a gesture and call attention to his presence with some remark. Sometimes he will tend toward a harsh swagger and over-consciousness of pride....

Bateson goes on to say that, among other factors, a man acquires prestige "by playing up to the public eye; the more standing he has, the more conspicuous will be his behaviour. The greatest and most influential men will resort freely to either harsh vituperation or to buffoonery when they are in the centre of the stage, and reserve their dignity for occasions when they are in the background."

Like Bibi Netanyahu, the Melanesian Big Man would never publicly admit to his mistakes, would never appear to be weak, and would never change his mind. A Big Man would never cancel a speech in the ceremonial house, which is not unlike the US Congress, an institution that is filled with the exaggerated behaviors of blustery and bombastic Big Men.

Should a Big Man be entrusted with power? Should he be entrusted with the responsibilities of war and peace, of life or death? My Songhay friends from the Republic of Niger, many of whom are masters of practical wisdom, are very conscious of the personal challenges and obligations of possessing power. They would call someone like Bibi Netanyahu a *bonberiko* (literally, the owner of a big head). If you observe a *bonberiko*, you quickly realize that despite the large size of his head, there is little of substance inside. When you entrust someone with power, they would say, you want a person who is calm and even-tempered, a person who thinks long and hard before making a decision, a person who speaks with careful deliberation, a person who understands the complex mesh of social relations, a person more like Barack Obama than Bibi Netanyahu.

CHAPTER SEVEN

THE ANTHROPOLOGY OF TRUMP: MYTH, ILLUSION, AND CELEBRITY CULTURE

[MARCH 2016]

Yesterday, millions of American voters cast presidential primary ballots on Super Tuesday. In a political season that has confounded political pundits whose judgment has been consistently flawed, Donald Trump, as was expected, had a big night, pushing ever closer to the Republican presidential nomination. Mr. Trump has steadfastly defied the expectations of so-called conventional wisdom in which a presidential candidate is cool, calm, and knowledgeable—a person who knows how to carry himself or herself with a good measure of dignity. Again and again, Donald Trump has challenged our "conventional" presidential expectations. Even as powerful members of his own party, like Speaker of the House Paul Ryan, repudiate him, Mr. Trump's support has ironically grown stronger and stronger.

What's going on in America?

Can we explain this strange and troubling turn of political events?

There are a variety of political explanations. Pundits have discussed any number of reasons for the success of Mr. Trump—repercussions of income inequality, a sense of hopelessness, the celebration of ignorance and the denigration of science, the perception that the political system, in the words of Senator Bernie Sanders, is "rigged," the public reappearance of bigotry in the name of "Making America Great Again."

As an anthropologist, I see the rise of Trump from a cultural vantage. He is the embodiment of celebrity culture—a world filled with glitz, fantasy, and illusion. It is culture in which shallow perception is more valuable than deep insight. If you watch Donald Trump perform his *shtick*, you hear pretty much the same thing. Mr. Trump comes on stage, recites his poll numbers, insults his opponents, invites famous supporters to the stage to sing his praises, and then talks, without giving concrete factual examples, about how bad things are and how he's the man to make things better.

Each event is a tightly controlled theatrical production that is designed to reinforce the myth of Mr. Trump's fearless strength, his invincibility, and his inevitability—a real strong man. When he moves to the debate format, which is a bit less controlled, he continues to talk about our broken system and how everyone is incompetent— including his opponents who are low energy, little people of no consequence. At no point does his talk focus upon a program for action, the complexities of policy, or the intractability of social, political, and economic problems at home and abroad. As he stated last night at his victory event, which was staged to look like a presidential press conference, the solutions to our problems are simple because he knows how to negotiate, he knows how to bring jobs back to America, he knows how to deal with China, he knows how to get the wealthy Gulf States to contribute their fair share to the Syrian migrant crisis. No one is going to mess with him—or us.

In his pared-down "tell it like it is" language, Mr. Trump is convincingly entertaining. He is not yet the president, but is trying to play one on television. Although he seems ignorant of the social, political, and cultural complexities of world, not to forget the US Constitution, it doesn't matter, for he is operating in a fantasy world in which facts don't matter, in which "competent" people—actors all—can quickly solve difficult problems. In the fantasy world of television, problems are easy to solve. On television or on social media, it's easy to build a wall across the US-Mexico border and get Mexico to pay for it. In the vicarious mythic worlds of television, Facebook, and Twitter, it's easy for Mr. Trump, who has disparaged Muslims, women, gays, the physically challenged, and Hispanics, to claim—with conviction—that he will win their support. In this mythic world, it is easy for Mr. Trump, who insults his opponents—even opponents of his own party—to say that he will be a unifying force.

In the real world, Mr. Trump's willful ignorance, his undignified behavior, and his Islamophobia are both senseless and dangerous. In the mythic culture of celebrity, as Mr. Trump seems to well understand, black becomes white and lies become truth. It is a world in which there is no space for critical reflection or for intellectual nuance. Mr. Trump brilliantly understands the culture of celebrity as a world of illusion in which he can carefully develop his mythic image. In this world he is the strong man, the "truth-teller," the man who will unite a divided nation.

All of this symbolic manipulation works quite well in the culture of celebrity. It works well enough to convince millions of angry Americans to believe in the myth of Donald Trump. Despite substantial evidence to the contrary Mr. Trump's supporters believe his mantra: things are horrible and we need a strong leader—Donald Trump—to fix a broken system. In this illusory world, you don't really need to know that much about politics or the world or the US Constitution. In the mythical context of illusion, if you have the right attitude and a high degree of self-confidence, as does Mr. Trump, you can solve any problem.

Thinking about the future of our children and grandchildren, let's hope that it's not too late for us to discover that behind the wall of illusion that Mr. Trump has built, the emperor has no clothes.

CHAPTER EIGHT

THE RETURN OF THE PLAGUE: AN OPEN LETTER TO OUR STUDENTS

(NOVEMBER 2016)

Dear Students:

I write with some unwelcome news: the plague has returned to America.

The rats have crawled out of their holes and are swarming over our bustling cities and our sprawling suburbs. They have infested our peaceful small towns and our bucolic farms. They have spoiled our pristine pastures and meadows. I'm sure that you would prefer to receive better news, but I feel it is my professorial obligation to give you an idea of what to expect from this new round of the plague.

Maybe you feel that I'm being an alarmist or overly dramatic. But I've been around long enough to have seen and experienced the vile nature of the plague. You see, when I was coming up in the 1950s and 1960s the rats came after me—and many, many others. They taunted us with epithets. On several occasions, they physically attacked us just because we were different.

When the plague comes, social life is transformed. Even if you think you are one of the good ones—the good Muslim, the good Asian, the good Latino, the good African American, the good LGBTQ person, the good Jew, the good woman, or even a good ol' boy—sooner or later the rats will come after you. Their appetite for hate is insatiable.

If you don't believe me, consider what happened one day after the upset election of Donald J. Trump. In his recent *Verge* report, Sean O'Kane listed the following hate incidents:

- A swastika and the words "MAKE AMERICA WHITE AGAIN" were spray-painted on a baseball dugout in Wellsville, NY (pop. ~5,000). A black baby doll was also found with rope around its neck in an elevator on campus at Canisius College outside Buffalo, NY.—*The Buffalo News*
- A reporter for CBS North Carolina posted a photo of a wall in Durham, North Carolina where the words "BLACK LIVES DON'T MATTER AND NEITHER DOES [sic] YOUR VOTES" were spray-painted.—Derrick Lewis, CBS North Carolina
- A swastika and the words "Seig Heil 2016" were spray-painted on a storefront in South Philadelphia. The Anti-Defamation League issued an official statement in response to the incident, saying that "while we view this as an isolated incident, we cannot allow this behavior to become routine. Everyone has a role to play in combating bigotry—we must advocate, educate and investigate until hate is no longer welcome in our society."—Philly.com, The Anti-Defamation League
- Also in South Philadelphia, the words "TRUMP RULES" and "TRUMP BLACK BITCH" were spray-painted on an SUV.

According to "Hate Watch," which is maintained by the Southern Poverty Law Center (SPLC), "between Wednesday, November 9, the day after the presidential election, and the morning of Monday, November 14, the Southern Poverty Law Center collected 437 reports of hateful intimidation and harassment." The SPLC stated that

> [m]ost of the reports involved anti-immigrant incidents (136), followed by anti-black (89) and anti-LGBT (43). Some reports (8) included multiple categories like anti-Muslim and anti-immigrant. The "Trump" category (41) refers to

incidents where there was no clear defined target, like the pro-Trump vandalism of a "unity" sign in Connecticut. We also collected 20 reports of anti-Trump intimidation and harassment.

These ugly incidents, which are likely to increase exponentially during the Trump Administration, are signs of the plague's return. It is a return baited in large measure by the silences, words, choices, and behavior our president-elect! Such news dims the bright light of your future.

What can you do to combat the plague?

How can the light of your future be brightened?

When I confronted the plague as a young man, I took solace in the wisdom of a great work of literature, *The Plague (La Peste)* by the legendary Albert Camus. In this book, Camus described how the plague changed the lives of the people of Oran in Algeria. The Oran authorities were slow to appreciate the gravity of the situation even after thousands of rats had died in the streets, even after people began to sicken and die. Only when the death tally reached 30 people per day did the authorities finally recognize the severity of the situation. They quarantined the city.

The townspeople became depressed. Violence spread. Hoodlums looted city shops. People lost their husbands and wives. Babies died. Oran became utterly chaotic. Eventually, the rats returned to their holes and the plague retreated. In time, people reunited with their loved ones and reestablished and reinforced their ties of love.

For Camus, the plague comes and goes but can never be completely eliminated. *The Plague* is, of course, allegorical. Camus wrote his masterpiece in response to the rise and fall of Nazi Germany. The recent empowerment of hate groups in Europe and the overt bigotry of Donald J. Trump's presidential campaign underscores the timeless wisdom of Albert Camus. Is it any wonder that Trump's unexpected win unleashed a torrent of hate crimes directed at Muslims, Jews, African Americans, immigrants, the gay community, and women?

In these troubled times, what can you do?

Should you act like the elders of Camus's Oran and ignore the presence of plague in our midst?

Should you do nothing and let the plague spread?

Camus's message is clear. First you have to recognize the plague when you experience it. Second, you have to fight it back with all your resources. Third, once the plague retreats you need to be vigilant because given the right circumstances, it can always come back.

In the end, though, Camus's novel celebrates human resilience. Toward the end of the book he writes: "once the faintest stirring of hope became possible, the dominion of the plague was over." He goes on to say that love trumps hate. Once the plague has been beaten back, you know that "if there is one thing one can always yearn for and sometimes attain, it is human love."

The times are troubling and difficult, and the plague always gets worse before it gets better. In time the rats will go back into their holes, the plague will retreat, and you will realize fully the power of love to overcome hate.

Sincerely,
Your professor

CHAPTER NINE

REVISITING THE ANTHROPOLOGY OF TRUMP: ANTHROPOLOGY AND THE POWER OF CULTURE

(NOVEMBER 2016)

Two days ago, the election of Donald J. Trump as our 45th president shocked millions of Americans. How could a man so seemingly ignorant of foreign affairs or, for that matter, the workings of government become the most powerful person in the world? How could so many scholars, pundits, and big data number crunchers fail to detect Mr. Trump's groundswell of enthusiastic support—especially in rural America? How could all those millions of Trump supporters take seriously his fact-free assertions about crime, climate change, the economic power of tax cuts, or the effectiveness of torture?

The deceptively simple response to these questions is **culture**, which, among other things, shapes our interpretation of reality.

In March of this year, I published a *Huffington Post* blog, "The Anthropology of Trump: Myth, Illusion, and Celebrity Culture." In that piece, I tried to demonstrate how Mr. Trump had brilliantly manipulated the fundamentals of celebrity culture—glitz, illusion, and fantasy—to create a kind of alternative reality in which shallow perception is more appreciated than profound insight. In the mythic culture of celebrity, as president-elect Trump understands so well, lies become truth and conspiracies become convincing evidence that our system is "rigged." In the glitzy world of celebrity culture, as I wrote in March, "you don't really need to know much about the politics or the world or the US Constitution. In the mythical context of celebrity culture, if you have the right attitude and a high degree of self-confidence, as does Mr. Trump, you can solve any problem."

If you have not experienced this alternative universe of meaning, how can you understand the powerful allure of Donald J. Trump?

In celebrity culture the contest between a star and a technocrat is no contest at all.

And yet in the 2016 election cycle, scholars, pundits, campaign professionals, and big data number crunchers overlooked these fundamentally powerful cultural issues. Blinded by their own cultural assumptions, the media and the political establishment overlooked the power of culture to shape an election. How many of them understood the social and psychological dynamics of the disaffected Trump voter? How many of them could understand their social frustrations, their lack of hope, or their embrace of a fictive reality?

We live in trying times that require anthropological input to combat the coming onslaught of Trumpism—the loss of health insurance, increasing deficits, the inevitability of climate disasters, racial and religious intolerance, and the re-institution of torture. Anthropological insights can help us to change the narrative of Trumpism and reconfigure the American political landscape into one that values social justice and human dignity. Participating in protests may make us feel good, but if you don't have a culturally attuned and politically convincing narrative, there's little chance for real social and political change.

In this time of social and political malaise, here are some moves we can employ to gradually make things better:

1. **The Power of Ethnography**. Ethnographers spend a good amount of time with the people whose lives they attempt to describe. In so doing they develop relationships with their subjects. Over time those relationships produce bonds of trust, fostering mutual respect and a deep comprehension of the other's culturally contoured view of the world. An ethnographer of a community that

voted overwhelmingly for Mr. Trump would have known—unlike the pundits, political operatives, and most scholars—that there was broad, deep, and enthusiastic support for Mr. Trump's view of the world. They would have known that Mr. Trump had understood profoundly the social and economic pain of his supporters. They would have also realized how he had used the dynamics of celebrity culture to shape that pain into a powerful political narrative. In this age of social media and celebrity culture, old thinking no longer works. Ethnographic thinking, by contrast, enables us to understand social and political dynamics and use them to precipitate meaningful social change.

2. **The Power of Thick Description**. The late Clifford Geertz, one of the great anthropologists of the 20th century, coined the term "thick description." In thick description, ethnographers observe an event—a ritual, an election, or a pattern of voting—and attempt to describe the sinuous patterns of the event's economic, social, political, and cultural significance. Thick description embraces complexity. In the world of analytics, where practitioners reduce human behavior to abstract and distanced mathematical specificity, thick description provides the kind of social and cultural context that big data usually overlooks.

3. **The Power of Cultural Critique**. Using thickly described ethnography, we can engage in savvy, sustained, and powerful cultural critique, one of the social scientist's primary obligations. In cultural critique we use ethnographically contoured essays, films, and blogs to bring into relief the hidden, taken-for-granted dimensions of our social systems—dimensions that reinforce racial, ethnic, class, and gender inequities. In the end, cultural critique is a powerful way to underscore the accountability of anyone, including, of course, Mr. Trump. We can use it to configure a counter-narrative to Trumpism, a counter-narrative that can limit its forthcoming damage to our society and eventually bring about a more perfect union.

Now is the time for ethnographers to step up to the plate and communicate our powerful insights to our students and to the public. Now is the time to craft a powerful counter-narrative that will ensure a viable future for our children and grandchildren.

CHAPTER TEN

GOING PUBLIC: RESISTANCE IN THE AGE OF TRUMP

(JANUARY 2017)

In the post-truth world of Trumplandia there is a clear need for scholars to go public—as a form of resistance. This need is particularly acute in the social sciences, in which scholars attempt to make sense of the human condition. Why is there discrimination and hate and cruelty in the world? Why is income and social inequality so historically persistent? Why do people not act in their best interests? What are the social factors that lead to needless suffering and premature death? Why have our politics become so mean-spirited?

As the inauguration of Minority President Donald J. Trump is fast approaching, there has been a groundswell of support for mounting a resistance to his set of nasty, short-sighted, and discriminatory policy initiatives—initiatives that a majority of Americans appear to be against. One day after Minority President Trump's inauguration, there will be well-publicized public protests against his presidency—the Women's March on Washington as well as hundreds of Sister Marches Against Trump. Going back to the resistance of the 1960s, scholars have scheduled Inauguration Day teach-ins on some of our university and college campuses. Indeed, these troubled times compel scholars to wade into the unpleasantly turbulent waters of public discourse in order to resist oppression, violence, political bullying, and intolerance.

What can scholars do to resist Minority President Trump?

A group of anthropologists is planning a virtual read-in on Inauguration Day during which they will read and discuss a chapter in the late Michel Foucault's collection of College de France lectures—*Society Must Be Defended*. The two organizers of the read-in, Paige West and J.C. Slyer, discussed their idea in a recent blog published in *Savage Minds*, perhaps the most important platform for contemporary anthropological blogging. In the blog, they wrote:

> This lecture strikes us as very good to think with at this present point: it demands we simultaneously consider the interplay of sovereign power, discipline, biopolitics and concepts of security, and race. In light of the current sociopolitical situation where the reaction to activism against persistent racism has been to more overtly perpetuate racism as political discourse, we need to remember and rethink the role of racism as central to, rather than incidental to, the political and economic activities of the state....

They continue:

> ... While the latter part of this argument has been addressed by numerous scholars and activists who write and think about race, class, sexuality and inequality more generally—with clear and compelling arguments about how this is not a "new" political reality for many but rather a kind of contemporary culmination and re-entrenchment of the structures of power and oppression that underpin the entirety of the national political project—the former part of the argument has been allowed to stand with little critique. Do we need to change what we do and not just how we do it? Not necessarily.

> ... We worry that by focusing on needing to change what we are doing and how we are doing it we lose sight of what we already do really well. We work to understand the world

through research, teaching, writing and reading. Along with this, we produce knowledge that allows others to under-stand the world and to work to change it.

The idea for a virtual read-in is an important one at the beginning of the Age of Trump. As West and Slyer rightly note, scholars should continue to do what they do: conduct rigorously designed research, read widely, think critically, and produce authoritative "knowledge that allows others to understand the world and work to change it."

Here's the rub. If that knowledge is produced but not consumed, it will have little impact on the quest for global social justice. Are research, thinking, reading, and producing texts like the aforemen-tioned blog going to make a difference in Trumplandia? Reading Foucault might provide a road map for resisting Minority President Trump, but the real work of resistance is down in the trenches—organizing, making phone calls, and printing flyers. For scholars, the work of resistance also means constructing a sustained social critique in op-ed pieces, in blogs, in films, in poetry, in drama, and in multime-dia installations—all in a language accessible to the general public.

The Inauguration Day Foucault read-in is a great idea. Once it's over I would urge those committed reader-scholars to sign up for workshops that will enable them to transform their rigorously derived and powerful insights into texts that will inspire their aunts, uncles, mothers, fathers, brothers, sisters, daughters, and sons.

That makes for a more formidable resistance.

CHAPTER ELEVEN

WHO IS THE ENEMY OF THE PEOPLE?

(MARCH 2017)

This morning I put on my gym clothes, hopped in my car, and drove to my local Jewish Community Center (JCC) for a Monday morning workout. As I approached I noticed two police cars had barricaded the entrance. I rolled down my window. A police officer approached me waving his hand.

I showed him my JCC card.

"The JCC is closed," he said.

"An incident?" I said, hoping that my suspicions would be wrong.

He nodded.

"This is unbelievable," I told him. "I'll turn around and go home."

A quick glimpse at my smartphone confirmed my suspicions. As reported by the Philadelphia affiliate of NBC, a bomb threat forced the evacuation of the Siegel JCC. As of noon, according to Brittany Horn of the *Wilmington News Journal*, "programs have resumed following yet another bomb threat at the Siegel Jewish Community Center in Talleyville."

The previous day antisemitic vandals desecrated 75–100 graves at the Mount Carmel Jewish cemetery in the Wissinoming section of

Philadelphia. Various public officials condemned these antisemitic acts, which have increased exponentially since the election of Donald J. Trump, whose responses to antisemitism and Islamophobia have been tepid, insufficient, or non-existent. Here's how the Anne Frank Center reacted to the recent wave of antisemitic acts in Philadelphia: "Jewish graves in Philadelphia now vandalized. Stop this incubator of #Antisemitism and other hate. WE BEG YOU @POTUS @realDonaldTrump." They went on to write:

> We are sickened, sickened, sickened. More Jewish gravestones were found vandalized today, this time in Philadelphia. Mr. President, it's time for you to deliver a prime time nationally televised speech, live from the oval office on how you intend to combat not only #Antisemitism but also Islamophobia and other rising forms of hate.

For me, this news is a back-to-the-future moment. I grew up in an era during which Americans practiced antisemitism much more openly. Back then housing covenants existed to prevent Jews from moving into certain neighborhoods. As a consequence, Jewish people often lived in enclaves to protect themselves and their children from the ever-present threat of antisemitic abuse. Despite this isolation, I, like many Jewish children of that era, experienced antisemitism, especially at the public schools I attended. Kids on the bus liked to make fun of my larger than normal nose and called me "dirty Jew." In junior high, a gang of classmates forced me into the bathroom and pushed my head into a toilet and flushed it.

"Not even that," one of them said, taunting me, "will clean you up, you dirty kike."

I picked myself up and faced them. They pointed at me and laughed.

"If you tell on us we'll beat you to a pulp, Christ killer."

I said nothing. They left. I dried my head, and wondered how I would make my way through the rest of my secondary schooling.

That day set the foundation of my social resilience, which has given me the courage to move forward in a wide variety of challenging circumstances here in America as well as in Europe and West Africa.

Since that fateful day, I experienced other acts of antisemitism, but as time passed they became less intense and much less frequent. I would always be "different," but perhaps I would learn to swim in the American mainstream. Eventually I made my way to college, the Peace Corps, and graduate school, where I studied anthropology, a discipline with a long history of combating racism and ethnic and religious intolerance.

Anthropologists have long critiqued beliefs in cultural superiority. In a climate of profound racism and ethnic bias, Franz Boas, the founding father of American anthropology, once wrote: "The existence of any pure race with special endowments is a myth, as is the belief that there are races all of whose members are foredoomed to eternal inferiority." In the early part of the 20th century Boas spent much of his professional life demonstrating the conceptual and evidentiary weaknesses of scientific racism and religious intolerance. Indeed, subsequent anthropologists have built an ethnographic record that demonstrates that "others" have much to teach us about living in the world.

As the recent uptick of hateful acts suggests, however, the scourge of racism, ethnic discrimination, and religious intolerance is still with us, and President Donald Trump remains morally disengaged from the social poison of his candidacy, which, lest we forget, was based upon messages of divisive hate. His presidency has unleashed the desecration of Jewish graves, the killing of an innocent immigrant in Kansas, the vandalism and firebombing of Mosques and African American churches, and the airport detentions of people who are black or brown or have the "wrong" names or practice the "wrong" religion.

This profoundly disturbing set of events can be linked to Trump's silent response to white nationalist antisemitism, ethnic intolerance, racism, and Islamophobia—the core principles of his presidential campaign, which solidified his base of support—a support based in large measure on messages of hate.

Is this what Americans have become in the alternate reality of Trumpism?

At this crossroads of American history, it is hard to know what the future holds. It is powerfully clear that no set of "alternative facts" will alter the ever-increasing demographic diversity in America, which in coming generations will become more and more profound. And yet, President Trump refuses to see the world—or, for that matter, our society—as it is. This disconnect, which has brought us back to the future of openly expressed hated, is likely to undermine the American social contract.

Who is the enemy of the people?

If hate is the result of "taking our country back," there won't be anything left to take back. The time for complacency is over. Hate is spreading far and wide. It's time to take to the streets. It's time to resist.

CHAPTER TWELVE

BUDGETING SOCIAL DARWINISM

[MARCH 2017]

There has been much chatter about President Trump's proposed "America First" budget as well as the roll-out of Trumpcare, which has been designed to replace the Affordable Care Act. Beyond the debatable specifics of these budget and health care proposals, it is clear—at least to me—that they reveal a disturbing back-to-the-future philosophy that applauds the American Social Darwinism of the early 20th century. To an anthropologist who has been thinking about the dynamics of culture and society for more than 30 years, these proposals are nothing less than a blueprint to restructure our society into a social organism, to cite President Trump's favorite classification scheme, of winners (the fit) and losers (the unfit), the latter of which will eventually weaken, sicken, die, and disappear, ensuring a fine and pure social life for all the winners.

Who are the winners and losers in Trumpcare and the America First budget?

Some of the winners:

- the young, the healthy, and the white, who are Christians;
- the corporate elite (also white and Christian, for the most part);

- White Nationalists, racists who want to return America to a pure state (white and Christian);
- the military-industrial complex, which will be showered with billions of dollars of additional funds.

In the context of Social Darwinism, the winners protect us from the losers who, if left alone, will pollute and weaken a pure society. That's what it means to "take our country back."

Some of the losers:

- the old, whose programs like Meals on Wheels are no longer "productive";
- the poor, who will lose their health insurance and heat subsidies;
- the infirm of all ages and backgrounds, who will also lose their health insurance and no longer be a "burden" to society;
- immigrants—especially Muslims and Hispanics—"terrorists and rapists," who are "bad people";
- African Americans, genetic polluters who threaten "our way of life";
- all people of color, also genetic polluters who speak and behave differently;
- Jews, who dare to practice openly a non-Christian religion and operate Jewish Community Centers;
- scientists, speakers of inconvenient truths—on climate change, for example;
- social scientists, who engage in social and cultural critique;
- artists and humanists who seek to understand the human condition to make life sweeter for everyone;
- journalists, who attempt to rebut an avalanche of "alternative facts."

The philosophy that shapes the America First budget and Trumpcare proposal underscores the notion of "personal responsibility." If you're poor or unemployed, you must be lazy or "unfit." Don't blame your misery on the rich or on the structural forces that have created and reinforced social inequality. If you work hard, you can be rich. If you don't, then you'll be poor and it's your fault. This line of thinking, in fact, channels Lionel Barrymore's Mr. Potter in Frank Capra's classic film *It's a Wonderful Life*, a film that mirrors our contemporary debate about social class, social fitness, and the social contract.

Beneath the surface of this reactionary rhetoric lies a troubling pattern that underscores the Social Darwinist notion that the rich—or the strongest and fittest—should be socially viable, while the poor—or the weakest and least fit—should be allowed to wither and die. Loosely based upon Darwin's theory of natural selection, Social Darwinists always want nature to take its rightful course in society. In the past, the rich and powerful used Social Darwinism to deny workers a decent wage, bash labor unions, and justify the refusal of the economic elite to help the poor. The poor were "unfit" and not worthy of help.

Let the market do its work. Don't blame the rich for your problems! Blame yourselves for being unemployed. Let nature take its course.

Doesn't that sound like Tea Party rhetoric? Doesn't that echo the rhetoric of candidate Trump? Doesn't this set of ideas give shape and substance to the America First budget and the Trumpcare proposal?

Before the Great Depression, Social Darwinist beliefs not only expanded American social inequality but also prompted the eugenics movement, which inspired programs in which the genes of the "unfit" were "cleansed" from society. Belief in eugenics compelled many American state legislatures to pass laws that sterilized "unfit" people. Inspired by eugenic theories, the US Congress passed a series of Immigration Restriction Acts in the 1920s. These laws severely limited or barred the immigration of peoples deemed "unit." Fit people came from Northern Europe. They were the winners. Unfit people came from Asia, or Eastern or Southern Europe. They were the losers. The American eugenics movement, of course, inspired the Aryan nationalism of Nazi Germany that resulted in the Final Solution and the "cleansing" of six million "unfit" Jews.

That was the horrific past. In the present it seems preposterous that American society might return to a past of scientific racism, anti-immigrant prejudice, and severe social inequality. But from my anthropological vantage, which has been shaped by generations of anthropological opposition to the racism and religious intolerance that fueled American Social Darwinism, that's what the America First budget and Trumpcare is all about.

If we do not resist Trump's social engineering with every fiber of our being, we will not only drift back to a reconfigured form of 19th-century economic royalism, but also return to the winner-loser ideology of Social Darwinism. Such a return will tear our society apart.

PART TWO

BLOGGING SOCIAL SCIENCE: THE CHALLENGE OF GOING PUBLIC

INTRODUCTION

Public blogs can shed light on the power of the social sciences to make sense of contemporary social and cultural life. In a culture of speedy irrevocable change, public blogs on social science practices can affirm the capacity of social science to shed light on the complex challenges we face in contemporary society. Communicating slowly developed social science concepts on fast social media platforms can lead to deeper public comprehension of the social challenges we confront.

Even so, many people think that the social sciences are superfluous. Indeed, these are hard times for the social sciences. In a climate of severely reduced budgets for higher education, the social sciences have been particularly hard hit. Many American state legislators, who control the purse strings for public higher education budgets, think that social science is a waste of taxpayer money. Why invest, they argue, in programs that do not train students for good-paying jobs? Applying an ever-expanding business model to higher education, these legislators want to invest in education programs (science, technology, engineering, and mathematics) that they think provide a good return on educational investment. In this climate, as we shall see in Part Three: Blogging Higher Education, university and college education becomes tantamount to technical job training—the very antithesis of a broadly based liberal arts education in which the social sciences play a central role.

Such politically induced intellectual turmoil in which welders are praised at the expense of ridiculed philosophers has expanded space for an ignorant critique of social science methods—especially the qualitative methods that are central to ethnographic practices. Social science blogs contribute deep counter-arguments to these shallow critiques. Given the limitations of most journalistic reporting, it is imperative that social scientists demonstrate why it is important—politically and socially—to use social science to provide depth and breadth to debates about politics, terrorism, social class, race, and climate change.

Blogging about social science on social media platforms is therefore an important element of public anthropology. It can help to remove social science from the shadows of public debate. Blogging social science can demonstrate the utility of ethnography, for example, to add flesh to the bones of policy debate. It is also a way to display how storytelling can impact public opinion.

Composing public social science blogs differs somewhat from political blogging. In some cases, social science bloggers write in response to some kind of public controversy—the impact of Florida Governor Rick Scott referring to the uselessness of anthropology (see Chapter 13), or the caustic methodological critique of Alice Goffman's *On the Run*, a critique of the veracity of qualitative social science (see chapters 18 and 19). In other cases, social science blogs can demonstrate the ramifications of shifting social science practices. "Slow Anthropology in the Age of Trump" (see Chapter 22), for example, is a reflection on how anthropologists might confront the existential exigencies of fast culture in the age of social media.

Writing social science pieces for *HuffPost* is not that different from composing public political blogs. The texts that work well feature sentences are short, snappy, and, whenever possible, in active voice. The length still needs to be around 850 words. In blogs about social science, however, there's more room for narrative—stories about the face of poverty encountered on a Greyhound bus in rural Georgia (see Chapter 14), or even posts about the power of narrative (see Chapter 16). In all of these posts the ultimate goal is to underscore the social and political importance of public social science scholarship in contemporary popular discourse.

To quote the title of a conference at the University of Durham (October 2017), public blogging about social science can demonstrate "Why the World Needs Anthropologists." My hope is that the following pieces from *HuffPost* demonstrate a productive way to write public blogs about social science.

CHAPTER THIRTEEN

THE LIMITED GOOD OF RICK SCOTT'S ANTHROPOLOGY

(OCTOBER 2011)

The ghoulish governor, Florida's favorite son, Rick Scott is in the news again. This time he's bashing anthropology and showcasing his profound ignorance of culture and society. "If I'm going to take money from a citizen to put into education then I'm going to take money to create jobs," Scott said earlier this week. "So I want the money to go to a degree where people can get jobs in this state. Is it a vital interest of the state to have more anthropologists? I don't think so." Later in the interview, Scott, whose daughter majored in anthropology at the College of William and Mary, said: "It's a great degree if people want to get it. But we don't need them here."

As you might expect, these comments triggered a torrent of critical commentary from anthropologists and others in the academy. Virginia Dominguez, the president of the American Anthropological Association, called Scott's comments "shortsighted" and "unfortunate" and requested a meeting with the governor so that he might be better informed about the usefulness of anthropology. Rachel Newcomb, who teaches anthropology in Florida, has written about the positive social and economic impact of anthropology in Florida.

She also discussed—quite powerfully—the perils of technocratic culture and how universities in China and India are attempting to incorporate anthropology and other liberal arts disciplines into their rather sterile curricula—all to train technologically informed students in critical and creative thinking. In a *Mother Jones* article about Governor Scott and anthropology, Adam Weinstein suggests that eliminating programs in anthropology and psychology would bring a political bonus for Governor Scott. He says that Scott may be out to eliminate anthropology and the liberal arts:

> As opposed to conservative-friendly disciplines like economics and business management, liberal arts produce more culturally aware and progressive citizens, inclined to challenge ossified social conventions and injustices. Eliminate cultural and social sciences from public colleges, and you'll ultimately produce fewer community organizers, poets and critics; you'll probably churn out more Rotarians, Junior Leaguers, and Republican donors.

Somehow I don't think that this waterfall of critical commentary will impress Florida's increasingly unpopular Tea Party governor. Even if he agreed to meet with officials from the American Anthropological Association, which is highly doubtful, their statements of fact would not convince him to change his mind. I'm not sure he cares what universities in China and India are doing to incorporate anthropology and other liberal arts disciplines into their curricula. Although he might not like the gist of the Adam Weinstein's piece in *Mother Jones*, he probably won't read it. If he did, he wouldn't give Weinstein's comments a second thought.

Governor Scott is an ideologue completely isolated from thoughts that fall beyond the boundaries of his disturbingly narrow view of the world. He makes harsh comments about anthropology and the liberal arts because he knows that they tap into the long-flowing stream of American populism. He knows that Americans pride themselves as a "can do" people. When there is a problem, real Americans find common-sense solutions. Fancy theories only get in the way of real results. Eggheads and pointy-headed intellectuals are effete. If they manage to do the job, they don't do it well. We don't need our children studying superfluous subjects like anthropology, psychology, music, and philosophy.

This set of ideas about common sense had an impact on my life. When my mother learned that I wanted to study philosophy in college, she became upset.

"What kind of job can you get with that?" she asked me.

"Well," I told her, "I want to be a writer."

"There's no money in that. You should be a doctor, a lawyer, or an accountant."

Not many people in my family had gone to college and those who did became—you guessed it—doctors, lawyers, and accountants. Much to my mother's dismay, I graduated college with a degree in philosophy and headed off to West Africa as a Peace Corps volunteer. But my mother, a spirited woman, was persistent.

"When you get back from Africa," she said as I departed for my two-year tour of Peace Corps service, "I'll arrange for you to see your cousin Ivan. He's in insurance and doing very well."

My late mother was a wonderful woman, but her experience of privation during the Great Depression made her view of the world a narrow one. She couldn't imagine her son becoming a university professor or a writer of books. Like millions of other Americans, including Governor Rick Scott, my late mother believed in the limited good.

The anthropologist George Foster coined the term "limited good" in 1965 to describe Mexican peasants who believed that the good things in life—money and good fortune—were in short supply and beyond their capacity to capture and fully enjoy. As a consequence, these peasants did not pursue new opportunities and lost their ability to dream about a different life.

My sense is that the notion of the limited good should not be restricted to the Mexican peasants that Foster so ably described. Belief in the limited good has long been part of mainstream American society, which means that politicians like Rick Scott have repeatedly tapped into these sentiments for political gain. My students, many of whom come from families of modest means, feel the pressure of the limited good. Their parents want them to major in business, accounting, or computer science—degrees that will lead to good, well-paying jobs. Who can fault them for wanting what's best for their kids? And yet many of my students, who have little or no interest in accounting, end up learning how to do audits instead of following their passion into anthropology, history, or psychology.

"I want to major in anthropology," one student said to me last week, "but my mom thinks it won't get me a job."

"My dad," another particularly brilliant student said to me, "thinks that anthropology is a waste of time."

"And what do you think?" I ask.

"I want to become an anthropologist."

"Then follow your heart and your passion," I told her. "I don't know if you'll succeed, but at least you will have tried. I'll help you in any way I can."

If we eliminate the liberal arts and humanities from public university curricula, we will produce a generation of uncritical technocrats who will have lost their sense of wonder, their feeling of intellectual passion, and their capacity to dream about life beyond the boundaries of the limited good. In such a passionless and unimaginative space, we will lose our capacity to think, grow, and reconfigure a rapidly changing world.

Is that what you want, Governor Scott? Is that what you want for your daughter and your grandchildren?

CHAPTER FOURTEEN

THE FACE OF POVERTY IN AMERICA

(FEBRUARY 2012)

It's not hard to see the face of poverty in America. You can see it on any street in just about any town—homeless people who sit on park benches, poor people who line up at the food pantry, or out-of-work people who wait for hours in the unemployment office. Even if we encounter poverty, we usually choose not to see it. Better to close our eyes than to think about the suffering of the poor.

Like many Americans, I would place myself in this closed-eye category. There are homeless people who "hang out" on the benches in the center of the university town where I teach. When I drive through town, I sometimes pass by the line of people at the local food pantry. At the grocery store, I sometimes find myself behind folks who are paying with food stamps. It is a disarming confrontation, which I, like most of us, have usually wanted to repress.

That changed one day almost two years ago in Atlanta, Georgia.

I needed to get from Atlanta, where I had just attended an academic conference at Emory University, to Asheville, North Carolina. Flying from Atlanta to Asheville would have been too cumbersome and too expensive. Choosing not to rent a car, I decided to be adventurous and take a Greyhound bus that cost only $49 for a one-way ticket.

When you take a Greyhound bus it is difficult to close your eyes to the face of poverty in America.

At the end of the conference, the university provided a van to drop me off at the airport or other points of departure.

"I'm going to the Greyhound bus station," I told the driver.

"You sure you want me to take you there?" the driver asked.

"I am."

When we got to the seedy location of Atlanta's Greyhound bus terminal, I noticed two armed security guards flanking the entrance.

The driver looked at me, a middle-aged, bespectacled professor wearing a navy blazer over jeans and a dress shirt.

"You sure you want to get out?"

I got out and entered a new world in which my first experience was to wait 45 minutes in the terminal. Most of the people there were either African American or Latino. The bathrooms were labeled "Men," but also "Caballeros," and "Women," but also "Damas." Two Spanish-speaking employees stood behind a stand marked "Information" to inform passengers about fares, bus policies, and schedules.

After about 30 minutes of waiting, a fight broke out between an older African American man and an African American woman of a certain age. After they made a lot of noise and landed a few blows to their respective bodies, the armed security guards escorted them out of the terminal. Fifteen minutes before departure, the passengers on my bus began to line up to get a good seat. Five minutes before departure, a terminal door opened and we followed a path to the bus. After showing our tickets to the driver, we got on the bus and found our seats. After everyone was on the bus, the driver went back to the terminal to collect paperwork. He locked us inside.

"You can't be too careful around here," he said as he locked the door.

The majority of the passengers, most of whom were going to Greenville, South Carolina, were youngish Latinos or African Americans. One woman was from Nigeria. Another passenger was an elderly Chinese woman who, like me, was en route to Asheville. None of them looked prosperous. All of them were eager to leave downtown Atlanta.

And so we did. The bus followed the local rather than the express route, picking up passengers along the way. In Gainesville, Georgia, a Latino man gave his Anglo wife some cash for her trip.

"It's only $20," she complained. "How's that going to last me a week at my mama's?"

The man shrugged and said, "Say 'hello' to everyone for me and my brother."

Ten miles outside of Gainesville, the bus broke down in the middle of nowhere. The driver, a middle-aged African American man and a 20-year Greyhound bus veteran, phoned Atlanta to ask for a replacement bus.

"This bus is unsafe to drive," he announced. "They're going to send a replacement bus. I don't know how long it's going to take. Relax. We'll be on our way before you know it."

The passengers began to grumble in English, Spanish, Yoruba, and Chinese.

"How long is it going to take?" the Anglo woman from Gainesville asked.

"I've got important business," one young African American man said. "I can't be stuck here all day."

Passengers filed out of the bus onto a field where they made phone calls or smoked. After three hours of waiting, some of the passengers got angry and vigorously voiced their displeasure. The driver phoned the police, who showed up in a matter of minutes. The police officers could have been straight out of Central Casting for *In the Heat of the Night*—tall, round, khaki-uniformed, blonds with crew cuts and wearing mirrored aviator sunglasses. They immediately zeroed in on the young African American males, demanding identification and prison histories.

"Yeah, I got out six months ago, but my record is clean," one of them told the officers. "You can check it out."

"There's no reason to act rowdy," one of the officers said. "Calm down and everything will be okay."

"I'll be calm, officer," the young man said. "You've got my word. I don't need any trouble."

"Well, if I have your word," one of the officers said, smirking.

They left and the replacement bus arrived an hour later—after sunset. Somewhere between Gainesville, GA, and Anderson, SC, which is about as rural as it gets in Georgia, we stopped for food. Just about everyone in and around the convenience store was speaking Spanish.

Needless to say, I was going to miss my connection to Asheville. The driver told me that the next bus to my destination was in two days. As we pulled into Greenville, near midnight, I wondered if I was truly living in America. Experience had compelled me to look hard into the face of poverty.

Looking hard into the face of that poverty, you realize that many people can no longer afford to travel by air, train, or car. Looking hard into the face of that poverty, you realize that authorities continuously harass poor folks for identification and don't care about their schedules. They can wait. They don't work, so why should we make an effort to serve them with efficiency and respect? If they get angry about this lack of respect, call the cops or call for back-up. Looking hard into the face of poverty, you also realize that America has become a profoundly multilingual and multicultural society in which it has become increasingly difficult to live a productive life.

These truths, which stare us in the face, are difficult to confront. There is a structure to poverty in America—a structure so entrenched by outmoded ideas and cultural beliefs that it is unmoved by the blather of political "talking points."

This structure of poverty is a central element of the contemporary social landscape in America. If we are to progress as a society, it is important to understand its power and persistence.

That said, I wonder how many of our public officials have seen the face of poverty in America?

Maybe it's time for them to take a trip on a Greyhound bus.

CHAPTER FIFTEEN

THE SOCIAL LIFE OF MUSIC—IN MALI

(MAY 2013)

The recent silencing of music in Mali, once a wondrous place of musical vibrancy and creativity, carries social and political implications far beyond the borders of that remote country in West Africa. It appears the music scene in northern Mali, the birthplace of Ali Farka Toure's "African Blues," has been effectively shut down.

When Islamic militants took over large swathes of northern Mali they forced the local inhabitants, who tend to follow moderate Sufi approaches to Islam, to accept a reactionary Taliban version of the Prophet's religion. When they occupied Timbuktu, they destroyed the shrines of Sufi saints and attempted with partial success to destroy the priceless medieval manuscripts of Timbuktu's famed libraries.

Morality patrols enforced proper dress codes and monitored what people ate. Spies reported "seditious" or "sacrilegious" comments. The militants also banned music.

According to Sujatha Fernandes, writing in the May 19 edition of the *New York Times,*

> The armed militants sent death threats to local musicians; many were forced into exile. Live music venues were shut down, and militants set fire to guitars and drum kits. The

world famous Festival in the Desert was moved to Burkina Faso, and then postponed because of the security threat.

While French and Malian forces largely swept the militants from Timbuktu and other northern towns earlier this year, the region is a still a battleground. Cultural venues remain shuttered. Even more musicians in the north are leaving the country because they fear vengeful acts by the Malian Army, whom they accuse of discriminating against northern peoples. The music has not returned to what it once was.

To this anthropologist who has spent more than 30 years living among and thinking about the peoples and cultures of Sahelian West Africa, the death of music in Mali is a terrible cultural loss. As Fernandes suggests, music is the force that establishes and reinforces social relations among Sahelian peoples. Aside from playing musical instruments, usually the *kora* (the African harp) or the *ngoni* or *mollo* (the Sahelian lute), the griot appears at rituals like weddings to chant family genealogies or sing the verses of long cultural epics that recount the heroic glories of the past. As such, griots and their music not only link past to present, but also build bridges to the future, for their most fundamental charge is to make sure that cultural memories are not forgotten.

In the same *New York Times* piece, Fernandes made a powerful point:

> One thing that the events in Mali have taught us is that music matters. And the potential loss of music as a means of social bonding, as a voice of conscience and as a mode of storytelling is not just a threat in an African country where Islamic militants made music a punishable offense. We would do well to appreciate music's power, wherever we live.

Music is a pulse, an energy that wordlessly transports us back to the past, makes us sensuously aware of the present, and compels us to think about the future. As in other art forms—literature, sculpture, painting, and performance—music slips into the deep recesses of our being. Sometimes it moves us. Wherever it is performed, music enhances our humanity and enriches our social lives.

Why would anyone want to ban music, literature, sculpture, painting, or performance? The power of the arts has always been a threat to powerful elites. Plato sought to expel the artist from his *Republic*, for the artist threatened to steer people toward the emotions of the heart rather than the logic of the head. In the 13th century, conservative Muslim clerics, who followed a strict interpretation of Sharia law, condemned Konya's whirling dervishes, whose spiritual approach to Islam challenged the reigning Islamic orthodoxies of the time. The same scenario, of course, is being played out in Mali and other Sahelian West African nations.

The conflict between narrow-minded orthodoxy and open-minded creativity, of course, is ever-present in the politically charged cultural discourse of US politics. In the name of religious or market orthodoxy, conservative politicians have cut funding for the arts, humanities, and social sciences. In their view, artists and scholars often produce works that are wasteful, morally questionable, or downright offensive. Such work in the arts also raises questions that powerfully challenge a political orthodoxy that is based upon fictive principles. Republican governors are attempting to dumb down their public universities—by cutting the social sciences and humanities—to create what amounts to technical training centers that will supply local industry with skilled "follow-the-rules" workers. Congressional Republicans now want to second-guess the funding decisions of the National Science Foundation on projects about which they have little or no expertise.

When orthodoxy is used to declare war on music, the arts, the humanities, and the social sciences, we undermine the foundation of our society and diminish our humanity. In the absence of provocative art, music, and science, we deplete our souls and are forced to live in a place, like contemporary Mali, in which platitudes have sapped our imaginations, a place in which hope dissipates into the dry air.

The power of orthodoxy is great, but so is the force of the arts to contest it with new thoughts and innovations. The results of this fundamental conflict will shape the quality of our lives in the future.

CHAPTER SIXTEEN

NARRATIVE AND THE FUTURE OF THE SOCIAL SCIENCES

(DECEMBER 2013)

As we approach the end of another academic semester, the news from our college campuses has been filled with stories about the decline of the social sciences and humanities. Grant money is drying up. The dwindling numbers of students who want to major in something like philosophy or anthropology prompt fiscally conscious administrators to sharpen their budget-cutting knives. They don't want to support programs that can't spit out "job-worthy" students.

Wedged between the natural sciences and the humanities, the social sciences are a particularly easy target for disdain. Natural scientists often consider scholars of the social as being methodologically insufficient—not scientific enough. Humanities scholars, for their part, often consider social scientists as theoretically shallow. Such in-betweenness makes the social sciences the frequent subject of institutional attack. Who needs such an ambiguous and unproductive field of scholarship? Given such a battle-scarred turf, it is not surprising that social scientists sometimes seem desperate for some kind of academic validation—a quest that sometimes leads to increasingly esoteric debate and writing that few people can truly appreciate, let alone understand. Such esoteric practice, in turn, creates a perceived irrelevance that is fodder for political or administrative rebuke.

My discipline, anthropology, is no exception to this pattern in the social sciences. During the past 30 years, anthropologists have spent much of their time and effort fashioning anthropological theories. During those 30 years, I have witnessed the arrival and disappearance of many theoretical orientations (too numerous to name in this blog), all borrowed from disciplines like philosophy, cybernetics, sociology, biology, or cognitive science. No matter the source of conceptual inspiration, our theorists have valiantly attempted to tame the beast of social and cultural difference. Each orientation has generated much excitement in its turn and, like the life of a blog, has been eventually replaced by the "next new thing," which has its fleeting moment of fame only to dissipate into the intellectual ether. Such impermanence, which is the stuff of everyday life, can be disorienting. And yet, the rules of the academic game require a fast and furious mastery of each "next new thing," a mastery that generates research funding, book contracts, and prestigious academic positions. These days the pace of conceptual change is so fast that it makes your head spin.

Events at the recent meetings of the American Anthropological Association in Chicago reinforced these general impressions. Two densely packed panels introduced American anthropologists to the "next new thing in our discipline," "the ontological turn," a move, in part, to bring anthropology back to big questions like what is the relationship between nature and culture, between human beings and objects. Indeed, "the ontological turn" takes anthropological discussion into an arcane philosophical arena.

In a recent article, "Relativism and the Ontological Turn Within Anthropology," Martin Palecek and Mark Risjord, two philosophers, state that most followers of "the ontological turn" hone in on a society's most abstract categories, attempt to incorporate local ideas into anthropological theory, reject "representationalism," and adopt a stance called "perspectivism." Even though there seems to be much confusion about what "the ontological turn" means—and means for—anthropology, hundreds of scholars, young and old, packed into a ballroom to listen to a debate about these rather arcane philosophical ideas. As I overheard lingering buzz about "the ontological turn" in corridor conversations, I wondered if the most recent arrival of "the next new thing" would temporarily quench our anthropological need for intellectual validation.

I don't want to belabor the already belabored ontological turn, which, in fact, has something to contribute to anthropological and philosophical discourse, except to suggest that it too will fade away and be replaced by yet another theoretical scheme. While it is intellectually important to debate grand theory, the discussion, at least from my vantage, can sometimes become shortsighted. What will scholars or, better yet, educated readers think of "the ontological turn" 10, 20, or 50 years from now?

Refinement of social science theory is incontestably important, but does it not sometimes divert our attention from real-world problems—extreme social inequality, structures of violence, environmental degradation, the ethical contours of social relations, or the fleeting nature of human well-being in the world? Grand theory attracts institutional attention, but at what cost? Do these abstract notions, no matter their ephemeral explanatory power in the present, generate work that remains open to the world?

The power of anthropology and the social sciences is found, at least for me, in the narratives we put forward about the social conditions of people living in the world. In the social sciences, the books with legs are those that create a connection between writers and a diverse audience of readers. Such a connection is established not through a jargon-laden esoteric language, but through narratives that evoke themes that constitute the human condition.

A great book like Piers Vitebsky's *The Reindeer People* is a case in point. It consists of an interconnected series of narratives about the Eveny people of Siberia. Even though *The Reindeer People* may not have the contemporary allure of "the ontological turn," its powerful stories evoke deep themes (about the relation of love and loss, courage and fear, and suffering and well-being) more powerfully than any abstract treatise. By the end of Vitebsky's work, readers have a palpable sense of what it is like to live a different life in a far-off corner of the world—a real connection. Because of this palpable connection, *The Reindeer People* is a work that will be read, savored, and debated for many years to come; it teaches us what it means to live in the world.

It would be foolish to deny the institutional importance of onto-logical turns. They are certain to spark scholarly debate—an essential element in the development of the social sciences. Taking the long view, though, it is evident that the future empowerment of the social sciences lies in the valorization of theoretically informed narratives that connect writers and readers, that explore human difference in a way that makes a difference, that compel readers to think a new thought or feel a new feeling. Such work will place the social sciences in a more comfortably productive space.

Who among us, after all, can ignore the power and glory of a really good story?

CHAPTER SEVENTEEN

WELCOME TO THE ANTHROPOCENE

(NOVEMBER 2014)

We live in very troubled times—welcome to the Anthropocene, a new epoch during which human activity (industrial production and consumption) has provided us unparalleled wealth but also an unmistakable path toward potential ecological devastation. As Naomi Klein powerfully demonstrates in her new book, *This Changes Everything*, the structures of our political and economic systems, which are inextricably linked, are leading us toward irrevocable climate change and inconceivable social transformation.

During the Anthropocene, we have witnessed the ongoing destruction of war and the ever-increasing celebration of terrorist atrocities. During the Anthropocene, the stains of nativism and racism, both brought on by increasing ignorance and media malfeasance, have spread far and wide. During the Anthropocene, to put the matter bluntly, the unprecedented prosperity that human activity has generated has ironically resulted in widespread misery in the world.

In America, our Anthropocene politics have brought us increasing income inequality, which means that social divisions are becoming increasingly rigid. Such social rigidity means that our middle class is shrinking, which, in turn, means that the number of families living in poverty is expanding. It is well known that in the US, supposedly the world's wealthiest nation, roughly 49 million of our citizens experience "food insecurity." One in five American children are hungry. Indeed, according to the 2014 *Hunger Report*, one in seven American families rely on food banks to feed their children.

Poverty and expanding social inequality also means that these alarming trends are likely to reinforce the social isolation of the poor. If we don't think about the poor, if we ignore those who are different from us (the aged, the sick, the homeless, and minorities of every ethnicity and sexual orientation), our problems will disappear and our social world will once again become strong and vibrant. Such are the politics of so-called personal responsibility, in which the rich, who work hard, deserve the luxuries of safe housing, copious food, and superb health care, and the poor, who are lazy, pay the price for their "indolence." Such an ideology, which ignores history or any kind of social analysis, reinforces racism and ethnic discrimination. Such an ideology also celebrates ignorance and advocates the distrust of scientists who, based upon rigorous research protocols, put forward inconvenient truths. These rigorously researched insights challenge a market fundamentalism that reinforces a fundamentally skewed social order.

Consider the dramatically inconvenient statement that Naomi Klein showcases in her aforementioned book, *This Changes Everything*. "In the face of an absolutely unprecedented emergency," wrote James Hansen, past director of NASA's Goddard Institute for Space Studies, and Gro Harlem Brundtland, former prime minister of Norway, who are two serious players on the world stage, "society has no choice but to take dramatic action to avert a collapse of civilization. Either we will change our ways and build an entirely new kind of global society, or they will be changed for us." (p. 22)

Threatened by unprecedented climate change and intractable socioeconomic structures of exclusion, nothing seems to work. Consider the shameful racism of our criminal justice system in which cops get away with the murder of young black men like Michael Brown. Consider the apartheid of our economic system in which "who you know" has become more important than "what you know." Consider our hapless low-information political system in which our elected officials celebrate their ignorance of science and social dynamics as they wave the tattered flag of market fundamentalism.

Something has got to give.

For me, the politics of the Anthropocene is an anthropological challenge. In the Anthropocene, it has been human activity that has directed us onto a destructive environmental path. By the same token, human activity can also direct us toward more positive social ends.

Enter anthropology and anthropologists. Most of my anthropological colleagues have been passive rather than active players on the sociopolitical stage. In our discipline, the institution has long celebrated arcane theoretical contributions for which practitioners receive research grants and endowed chairs. These times require a shift in emphasis. Given the political, social, and ecological crisis we face, anthropologists are uniquely positioned to demonstrate in clear and concise language and image how market fundamentalism, which generates climate change, social inequality, racism, and the defamation of difference, has brought us to the social precipice. By moving from passive to active voice, anthropologists, among other cultural critics, can provide the insightful information needed to construct a groundswell of change—a course correction away from a path to social apocalypse.

Using a variety of social media that reach ever-expanding audiences, here's a sample of what active voice anthropologists can do:

1. Expand our blogs and documentary shorts and features about income and social inequality to demonstrate in plain language how economic exclusion is economically and socially counter-productive.
2. Expand our discourses on the exercise of power and how it is tied to the ideology of market fundamentalism.
3. Continue our critique of the corporatization of the social life—especially the corporatization of the university.
4. Continue our discourses on the destructive dynamics of racism and ethnic discrimination.
5. Broadcast the insights of science and social science, again in plain language, to demonstrate how and why they are trustworthy.

This cultural critique must be constant and consistent. As frustrating as such an exercise might be, we will need to restate and continuously refine our presentations so that our inconvenient insights will gradually convince people to change. In this way, we might salvage some degree of compassionate social life on the planet. At the same time, we should develop further an anthropology of well-being to demonstrate how to siphon off measures of mirth in increasingly trying times.

The Anthropocene presents to anthropologists and other social scientists a profoundly humanitarian obligation. As the Songhay people of Niger like to say: even though the path toward truth is long, it is one that is always worth taking.

Will we do our part to make the world a bit sweeter for our children and grandchildren?

CHAPTER EIGHTEEN

ALICE GOFFMAN AND THE FUTURE OF ETHNOGRAPHY

(JUNE 2015)

When scholars attract widespread public attention, the news coverage about them and their works, which is often incomplete and filled with misconceptions, is not usually good. So it is with the public controversy about Alice Goffman's much-discussed book, *On the Run: Fugitive Life in an American City*. Consider Marc Parry's recent *Chronicle of Higher Education* article, "Conflict Over Sociologist's Narrative Puts Spotlight on Ethnography." Here's some of what Mr. Parry wrote:

> Late last month, what began as a book review in an obscure publication blew up into a major controversy that tarnished sociology's most-buzzed-about young star. At issue: whether the sociologist, Alice Goffman, had participated in a felony while researching her ethnographic study of young black men caught up in the criminal-justice system.
>
> That claim brought Ms. Goffman back into the news, but the backlash against her had been building for months. Journalists and scholars had acclaimed her 2014 book, *On the Run: Fugitive Life in an American City*, as an ethnographic

masterwork, transforming a press-shy junior scholar into a TED-talking celebrity. But discussion of Ms. Goffman's book soon took on a more cutting tone, as reviewers questioned the accuracy of her portrayal of black life, the soundness of her methods, and the possibility that her book might harm its subjects.

The dust-up reveals anxieties that go beyond the censure of Ms. Goffman, opening a fresh debate over longstanding dilemmas of ethnographic research: the ethical boundaries of fieldwork, the tension between data transparency and subjects' privacy, and the reliability of one ethnographer's subjective account of a social world. Some sociologists worry that the controversy may put a chill on sensitive fieldwork. Others fear that it could damage the credibility of ethnography at a time when sociologists are being exhorted to get more involved in public debates.

It is curious that Mr. Parry didn't reach out for anthropological commentary on the ethical, textual, and methodological issues that Goffman's ethnography evokes. In so doing he ignored generations of anthropological debate about the whys and wherefores of doing ethnography—debates about ethics, transparency, the mix of narrative and analysis, as well as the complexities of doing—or not doing—"native" ethnography. In contrast to sociology, the practice of ethnography is the foundation of anthropological research and, as I see it, the centerpiece of anthropology. Ethnography is the fertile soil from which our comprehension of the human condition emerges. It is the basis for our contribution to public debate about important social and political issues like racism, income inequality, and climate change.

It is only fitting, then, to add some anthropological reflections to what has been largely a sociological and legal discussion of the Goffman kerfuffle.

After almost 40 years in the ethnographic trenches, it is clear to me that doing any kind of ethnography is a very messy business. When ethnographers set out to describe social relationships among a group of people, they must also build a complex web of relations between themselves and their subjects. Those relations are never straightforward. No matter where ethnographers might be—West Philadelphia,

Indonesia, Brazil, or West Africa—the emotional texture of those relationships invariably shapes the kinds of information that gets exchanged as well as the nature of the text that ethnographers eventually write. In ethnography, the personal and the professional are never separate, meaning that good ethnography is not likely to consist of bloodless prose. Put another way, doing ethnography, like living life, involves love and hate, fidelity and betrayal, and courage and fear. Sometimes ethnographic experience brings us to face to face with issues of life and death—the real stuff of the human condition.

Those relationships, as I can attest from my own research among sorcerers in the Republic of Niger and among West African immigrants in New York City, sometimes create ethical dilemmas that no research design, no theoretical argument, or no set of ethical guidelines can easily resolve. Like all scientific endeavors, ethnography involves a set of interpretations, the contours of which are shaped by personal disposition, theoretical and methodological training, and the intersubjective dynamics of the ethnographic setting, which consists of an ever-changing matrix of social relations and events that taxes our cultural desire to transform social chaos into some semblance of social order.

Confronted by emotionally taxing events, ethnographers are sometimes compelled to write against the disciplinary grain, invoking in their works the raw emotions of fieldwork. Ethnographic works that stray from the textual norm invariably draw varying degrees of trenchant critique. As in *On the Run*, against-the-grain ethnographers tell troubling stories and attempt to link those stories to larger social issues like the strained relations that exist between the police and African American men, or the sometimes violent acts that sorcerers enact against members of their own communities.

When ethnographers skillfully recount these kinds of stories, they usually open themselves to the world of their subjects, to the scrutiny of their colleagues and, of course, to the curiosities of their readers. In doing so, they expose their human vulnerability. They make mistakes, discuss their errors of judgment, and express their fears and misgivings. Such vulnerability, which is an important aspect of Alice Goffman's book, creates connections between the writer and the reader—the kind of connection that compels the reader to turn the page, pay attention, think a new thought or even feel a new feeling.

But can we trust ethnographic accounts? Can ethnographers get "it" right? Given the infinite complexities of the social laboratory, "the quest for certainty," as the philosopher John Dewey put it, is an illusion. If ethnographers cannot provide a perfect, scientifically verifiable representation of reality, how can anyone judge the contribution of an ethnographic work? This question, which has been raised by some of Goffman's critics, fails to fully appreciate the aim of ethnography.

The great power of ethnography lies in its capacity to describe places and people such that readers come to know something about life in Philadelphia's African American neighborhoods, or to learn something about the struggles of rural Songhay people living on the desiccated steppes of the West African Sahel, or to discover Eveny nomads who herd reindeer in the frozen expanses of Siberia. Description of these places and peoples leads not to eternal truth, but to what the late philosopher Richard Rorty called "edifying conversations," conversations that increase cross-cultural awareness in an increasingly integrated world.

It is not easy to write a book about gut-wrenching ethnographic experience. *On the Run*, we should remember, is Alice Goffman's first work. It is a gripping description of the social life of young African American men in one Philadelphia neighborhood—an aspect of social life about which most Americans have limited, if any, knowledge. Tangled in the web of that neighborhood's social relations, Goffman wrote *On the Run* through the lens of her own experience. Like any ethnography, especially a first book, *On the Run* has flaws that should be discussed.

Do these flaws diminish its ethnographic contribution?

The real test of an ethnographic work is whether it has legs. If it does, it becomes a text that remains open to the world. If it doesn't have legs, an ethnographic work, like so many academic texts, quickly fades into obscurity. Having witnessed many similar kinds of book controversies over the years, my suspicion is that the hot debate about *On the Run* will eventually become a cool discussion that will lead to insights that will reinforce the power of ethnography to shape future public discussion.

As for Alice Goffman, I look forward to her next book.

CHAPTER NINETEEN

IN DEFENSE OF ETHNOGRAPHY

(AUGUST 2015)

As students and faculty head back to college campuses to begin a new academic year, there has been a steady stream of uninformed criticism of the practice of ethnography, a method of inquiry and representation that has become an important aspect of social science research. The most trenchant criticism has come not from anthropologists or sociologists who have long practiced ethnography but from legal scholars or survey researchers who for the most part don't have hands-on ethnographic experience. The most recent critique of this sort comes from legal scholar Paul Campos, who last week used the pages of the *Chronicle of Higher Education* (CHE) to produce a 10,000-word essay that questions the ethics and veracity of Alice Goffman's acclaimed ethnography, *On the Run*. Goffman's ethnographic work describes, among many things, the dangerously tense relationship between the police and young African American men in one of Philadelphia's crime-ridden neighborhoods.

Mr. Campos faults Dr. Goffman's book for its implausibility—faulty time lines, narrative incongruities, and putatively embellished eyewitness descriptions of police behavior. He also claims that Dr. Goffman and her publisher are guilty of shoddy fact checking. According to Mr. Campos, many of the "facts" in Dr. Goffman's ethnography are bungled and/or fabricated—a very serious accusation. Based upon his own "fact checking," Mr. Campos wonders how such a flawed work could be so honored and acclaimed. This concern leads him to question the "plausibility" of ethnographic practice and representation. In a blog summary of his long CHE article, which non-subscribers cannot read, Mr. Campos concludes that the flaws of Goffman's book raise questions about how social science work in general, and ethnographic work in particular, is evaluated and rewarded. From the article:

> Science is often bitterly competitive but it depends on honesty. It is not set up to weed out liars. Imagine what research, or talks, or conferences would be like if you had to routinely question not simply the quality or competence but the actual honesty of speakers. The same goes for supervision. Consider having to check not just the quality of your grad students' work, but whether they were lying to you about their data. Much of what we do would become simply impossible.
>
> To which a skeptic might reply: If science is bitterly competitive, and it isn't set up to catch liars, and there are great rewards for liars who don't get caught, then one doesn't need a Ph.D. in social science to realize that this system will produce a whole lot of lying, and that a lot of that lying won't ever be discovered.

I haven't read Mr. Campos's scholarly essays, and as an anthropologist I would hesitate to critique work about which I have limited expertise. That said, I assume he is a well-regarded legal scholar. Having worked my way through his long CHE article, I can also say that he is very skilled at building an argument. Those admirable skills do not alter the fact that he is, as far as I know, not a practicing ethnographer who has conducted fieldwork and written ethnographic texts. Even so, he uses his critique of Dr. Goffman's book to suggest a pervasiveness of lying in the social sciences.

As an anthropologist who has been doing ethnography for more than 30 years in West Africa and New York City, I am compelled to bring into this critical discussion an edifying ethnographic voice.

In what remains of this blog post I briefly describe the practices of ethnography and how they are governed by an extensive code of ethics.

Ethnographic practices: Ethnographers engage in fieldwork. They don't visit people for a week or two or call them up on the phone and then write about them; rather, they live in their subject communities for long periods of time, often many years, during which they establish and reinforce a network of social relationships—relationships that underscore the complex social, economic, and emotional realities of contemporary social life. During fieldwork, ethnographers invariably interview many people, but they also participate in the lives of their subjects, developing an interpretative sensitivity that can only be acquired over long periods of time. A cardinal principle of ethnographic fieldwork is this: listen to what your subjects are saying, but pay special attention to what they do. As we all know, what a person says is not necessarily what he or she does. What a police detective might say to a fact checker about an arrest may be very different from how he or she might have behaved during that arrest. To make sense of the intersubjective complexity of contemporary social life, ethnographers need to spend a great deal of time "being there" to get a fuller and more nuanced picture of the people they want to describe. In short, ethnography takes a lot of time, some degree of courage, and much perseverance. Anthropologists, for whom ethnography is central, have been writing about these issues for more than 40 years.

Curiously none of the recent critics of ethnographic practices make reference to this rich and highly reflexive body of work.

Ethics: The critics also suggest that that social science institutions are set up to produce, as Mr. Campos writes, "a whole lot of lying, and … a lot of that lying won't ever be discovered." This statement suggests social science ethics are seriously compromised. A brief review of the American Anthropological Association (AAA) code of ethics, however, suggests a robust and profound commitment to ethics in ethnographic fieldwork. Here is snippet of that code:

> Anthropologists should be clear and open regarding the purpose, methods, outcomes, and sponsors of their work. Anthropologists must also be prepared to acknowledge and

disclose to participants and collaborators all tangible and intangible interests that have, or may reasonably be perceived to have, an impact on their work. Transparency, like informed consent, is a process that involves both making principled decisions prior to beginning the research and encouraging participation, engagement, and open debate throughout its course. Researchers who mislead participants about the nature of the research and/or its sponsors; who omit significant information that might bear on a participant's decision to engage in the research; or who otherwise engage in clandestine or secretive research that manipulates or deceives research participants about the sponsorship, purpose, goals or implications of the research, do not satisfy ethical requirements for openness, honesty, transparency and fully informed consent. Compartmented research by design will not allow the anthropologist to know the full scope or purpose of a project; it is therefore ethically problematic, since by definition the anthropologist cannot communicate transparently with participants, nor ensure fully informed consent.

Anthropologists have an ethical obligation to consider the potential impact of both their research and the communication or dissemination of the results of their research. Anthropologists must consider this issue prior to beginning research as well as throughout the research process. Explicit negotiation with research partners and participants about data ownership and access and about dissemination of results, may be necessary before deciding whether to begin research.

In their capacity as researchers, anthropologists are subject to the ethical principles guiding all scientific and scholarly conduct. They must not plagiarize, nor fabricate or falsify evidence, or knowingly misrepresent information or its source. However, there are situations in which evidence or information may be minimally modified (such as by the use of pseudonyms) or generalized, in order to avoid identification of the source and to protect confidentiality and limit exposure of people to risks.

The complete statement on such ethical elements as (1) doing no harm, (2) and being open and honest about one's work can be accessed on the AAA website, which also supports an ethics blog on which ethical issues, which are usually neither clear-cut nor easily resolved, are aired and debated.

None of this information, which is central to the practice of ethnography, is referenced in the recent critiques of ethnographic practices and representation.

The Power of Ethnography: It is much easier to critique an ethnography than to write one. Doing ethnography is difficult. It takes time. It demands patience. It requires diligence, sensitivity, commitment, and a foundation of mutual trust.

Through the ongoing social implication of the ethnographer in the lives of her or his subjects, these dimensions gradually develop. This painstaking and difficult process eventually enables the ethnographer to tell the story of a group of people with respect, power, and a depth of understanding that allows us to better understand the human condition. In these troubled times in which inhumane global forces threaten our future, we need that ethnographic depth of understanding both to recognize our human fragility and to marvel at our social resilience.

CHAPTER TWENTY

TERRORISM: A CHALLENGE FOR THE SOCIAL SCIENCES

(DECEMBER 2015)

We live in dangerous times. Our mean streets have become killing fields. During the past year police officers have shot and killed many unarmed African American men. During the past year, Christian terrorists have killed (1) nine innocent African Americans in a historic Charleston, South Carolina church and (2) a police officer and two innocents at a Planned Parenthood facility in Colorado Springs. During the past year, Muslim terrorists have slaughtered 130 Parisians in the City of Light and 14 innocent people attending a holiday gathering in San Bernardino, California.

What's the world coming to?

How can we come to grips with these senseless acts of violence—all too often in the name of religion?

Sadly, a common response to terrorism is bigotry and xenophobia. "They" are invading "us." "They" (who are always different from "us") are trying to kill "us," attempting to destroy our civilization. "They" must be stopped. If these statements seem far-fetched, consider the comments of Jerry Falwell, Jr. in response to the San Bernardino attacks, as reported in the *New York Post*.

> Liberty University president Jerry Falwell Jr. urged students
> Friday (December 4, 2015) to carry concealed weapons on
> campus to counter any possible armed attack, saying that
> "we could end those Muslims before they walk in..."
>
> "Let's teach them a lesson if they ever show up here,"
> Falwell told students at the Christian school.
>
> "I've always thought if more good people had concealed
> carry permits, then we could end those Muslims before they
> walked in," Falwell said.

Considering the ever-expanding cloud of Islamophobia in Europe and the US and the importance of the campus gathering, how likely is it that Mr. Falwell misspoke? Would the students there really think he was referring to a tiny percentage of the more than 1 billion Muslims in the world? Would Falwell consider Muslims carrying a concealed weapon to be "good" people?

Fueled by the recent terrorist events, xenophobia and bigotry have infected European and American political discourse. Following the terrorist attacks in Paris, Marine Le Pen's anti-immigrant, anti-Muslim political party, Le Front National, made significant gains in the recently concluded first round of French regional elections. In an equally xenophobic atmosphere, Republican presidential candidates, most of whom say we are at "war" with radical Islam, have now called for, among many things, carpet-bombing ISIS strongholds in Syria and Iraq, for "taking out" "their" families, for re-instituting the torture (waterboarding) of the "enemy," for increasing surveillance of mosques and social activity in Muslim neighborhoods, for accepting Christian but rejecting Muslim refugees from Syria, and, as of today, for a complete ban of Muslims entering the US.

This rhetoric is nothing less than ugly fearmongering to an increasingly fearful public. In such a climate of fear, many Americans may be willing to give up on the basic principles of our open society—freedom of speech, freedom of assembly, freedom of religion, and the right to privacy. These are the principles that prevent us from becoming a police state.

Indeed, there is an increasing segment of our society that would use the uncertainties associated with a pervasive climate of fear to throw out the separation of church and state and eliminate the secular foundation of our society. Writing in *truthdig*, Chris Hedges recently stated:

> Tens of millions of Americans, lumped into a diffuse and fractious movement known as the Christian right, have begun to dismantle the intellectual and scientific rigor of the Enlightenment. They are creating a theocratic state based on "biblical law," and shutting out all those they define as the enemy. This movement, veering closer and closer to traditional fascism, seeks to force a recalcitrant world to submit before an imperial America. It champions the eradication of social deviants, beginning with homosexuals, and moving on to immigrants, secular humanists, feminists, Jews, Muslims and those they dismiss as "nominal Christians"—meaning Christians who do not embrace their perverted and heretical interpretation of the Bible. Those who defy the mass movement are condemned as posing a threat to the health and hygiene of the country and the family. All will be purged.

The millions of people who adhere to this set of beliefs maintain an ideology that denies science, secularism, and religious difference. Considering the rhetoric of Donald Trump, Ted Cruz, Ben Carson, and Marco Rubio, this ideology has become an integral part of our political discourse. It is an ideology that feeds upon the celebration of ignorance and a distrust of reason. Although the texture of its expression may vary, this ideology—at its foundation—gives shape to a worldview shared by strange bedfellows: the Christian right and the Salafists of the Islamic State.

This potentially catastrophic culture of ignorance presents a profound challenge for the social sciences. In a time when the enemies of reason threaten the future of the sciences and the humanities, it is time for scholars to step up and be counted. It is time for us to become engaged in two domains: the public arena and the classroom. In the public sphere, we need to combat anti-reason with compelling and accessible accounts of how to confront a troubling world with a clear-sighted precision that accepts and works through the complex issues of our times—racism, income inequality, climate change, and terrorism. In the coming months, we need to be more prominent in the blogosphere, a space where our fears, passions, problems, and potential solutions can be articulated—a powerful force for reason in unreasonable times.

The second domain is in the classroom—a pivotal battleground in the assault against ignorance. Taking the long view, if we teach our students how to think critically and clearly, how to weigh the validity of evidence, and how to express themselves clearly and powerfully, they will stand on a foundation that will enable them to grow into engaged citizens in a vibrant, diverse, and tolerant society.

Four days ago, I gave the final lecture of my introductory course in cultural anthropology, during which I talked about immigration and cultural difference in American society. I ended the lecture with a discussion of Roger Sanjek's award-winning book, *The Future of Us All*, in which the author describes social and political life in the Elmhurst-Corona neighborhood of Queens, New York, perhaps the most culturally diverse space in the US. In the book Sanjek describes how, against all odds, the Elmhurst-Corona community managed to function successfully despite the many jagged lines of race, ethnicity, and language that cut across its social space. Considering unmistakable demographic trends in the US, it is clear that racial, ethnic, and linguistic diversity will shape our future society. Diversity and difference are, indeed, "the future of us all."

So, in an environment of terrorist threats, should we listen to the likes of Trump and Cruz and fear the expansion of difference and diversity?

Not at all.

It is worth repeating again and again that the increasing presence of racial, ethnic, and linguistic diversity will make our future a socially robust one. By the same token, it is worth repeating again and again that following the path of xenophobia and bigotry leads us to a bleak future of decline and decay.

In today's world the stakes are high, the path is long, and the challenge is great—time to dig in and continue the fight for science and reason.

CHAPTER TWENTY ONE

FAST CULTURE IN THE AGE OF TRUMP

(JUNE 2017)

In the Age of Trump, what are the political costs of our fast culture? Consider our fast politics. We have so much day-after-day political scandal—Russia, the firing of FBI Director James Comey, Trump's alleged abuse of power and obstruction of justice—that we become numb. Fast-breaking and scandalous news, I'm afraid, is the new political normal. In a speedy culture that affords us no time for reflection, our president doesn't even seem to know the details of the mean-spirited legislation or the arithmetically incorrect budget he has proposed. In our fast culture, Trump has little time to read or study detailed position papers, let alone daily briefing papers. Many of our legislators, also pressed for time in our speedy culture, don't read the legislation on which they are charged to vote. In the absence of time, though, there is the ever-present tweet and the possibility to reduce complex domestic or foreign policy to a mere 140 characters of time and space.

Fast culture, however, reaches far beyond the realm of politics. Each and every day we struggle to dig out from under an avalanche of texts, tweets, Facebook posts, and email messages. Videos go viral and people are "live" for one hour, or maybe even one day.

What are the social consequences of fast culture?

In an era of connectivity, we seem to become increasingly disconnected—from each other and from reality. In her important book, *Reclaiming Conversation: The Power of Talk in a Digital Age*, Sherry Turkle, a sociologist, argues that it is face-to-face, time-consuming, and unpredictable conversation that makes us human. "But these days," she writes on the first page of her book, "we find ways around conversation, we hide from each other even as we're constantly connected to each other.

Turkle goes on to discuss the social consequences of our fast-paced, media-saturated culture:

> We say we turn to our phones when we're bored. And we often find ourselves bored because we have become accustomed to a constant feed of connection, information, and entertainment. We are forever elsewhere. At class or at church or business meetings, we pay attention to what interests us and then when it doesn't we look to our devices to find something that does....
>
> We begin to think of ourselves as a tribe of one, loyal to our own party. We check our messages during a quiet moment or when the pull of the online world simple feels irresistible. (p. 4)

In fast culture, our online connection creates social disconnection. In fast culture, we are flooded with information and yet we seem to become more and more ignorant about the world of politics, culture, and social life. Consider a few of the disturbing items presented in Ray Williams's June 7 *Psychology Today* article, "Anti-Intellectualism and the 'Dumbing Down' of America."

• The Oklahoma Council of Public Affairs commissioned a civic education poll among public school students. A surprising 77% didn't know that George Washington was the first President; couldn't name Thomas Jefferson as the author of the Declaration of Independence; and only 2.8% of the students actually passed the citizenship test. Along similar lines, the Goldwater Institute of Phoenix did the same survey and only 3.5% of students passed the civics test;

- 18% of Americans still believe that the sun revolves around the earth, according to a Gallup poll;
- The American Association of State Colleges and Universities report on education shows that the US ranks second among all nations in the proportion of the population aged 35–64 with a college degree, but 19th in the percentage of those aged 25–34 with an associate or high school diploma, which means that for the first time, the educational attainment of young people will be lower than their parents;
- 74% of Republicans in the US Senate and 53% in the House of Representatives deny the validity of climate change despite the findings of the US National Academy of Sciences and every other significant scientific organization in the world;
- According to the 2009 National Assessment of Educational Progress, 68% of public school children in the US do not read proficiently by the time they finish third grade. And the *US News & World Report* reported that barely 50% of students are ready for college-level reading when they graduate;
- According to a 2006 survey by National Geographic-Roper, nearly half of Americans between ages 18 and 24 do not think it necessary to know the location of other countries in which important news is being made. More than a third consider it "not at all important" to know a foreign language, and only 14% consider it "very important";
- According to the National Endowment for the Arts report in 1982, 82% of college graduates read novels or poems for pleasure; two decades later only 67% did. And more than 40% of Americans under 44 did not read a single book—fiction or non-fiction—over the course of a year. The proportion of 17-year-olds who read nothing (unless required by school) has doubled between 1984 and 2004;
- Gallup released a poll indicating 42% of Americans still believe God created human beings in their present form less than 10,000 years ago.

As we sprint from topic to topic and scandal to scandal in our fast culture society, we become more and more isolated, alienated, ignorant, irrational, and angry. Fast culture seems to have set the stage for the election of our Tweeter-in-Chief, Donald J. Trump, who apparently doesn't read books or articles. In the Age of Trump, we increasingly celebrate our ignorance. In the absence of vital human face-to-face conversation, as Sherry Turkle points out, we lose our capacity for empathy, our ability to take the other's perspective. Turkle doesn't suggest we eliminate our reliance on digital technologies, but argues that we should approach social media from a different perspective. At the end of her book, she writes:

> We had a love affair with a technology that seemed magical. But like great magic, it worked by commanding our attention and not letting us see anything but what the magicians wanted us to see. Now we are ready to reclaim our attention—for solitude, for friendship, for society. (p. 361)

In a sense Turkle is suggesting that we all become anthropologists who, in their desire to understand other people, build empathetic relationships, all of which take time to develop. In this way, we build degrees of social trust, the foundation of the social contract. In the fast culture of the Age of Trump, perhaps it is time to slow down a bit, engage in conversation, and take the time to reclaim our humanity.

CHAPTER TWENTY TWO

SLOW ANTHROPOLOGY IN THE AGE OF TRUMP

(JUNE 2017)

In contemporary fast culture, we need a slow anthropology—for everyone. In the previous blog post I discussed how the spread of digital technologies and the pervasiveness of social media have presented us with a bevy of unintended social and political consequences. Increased online connectivity has resulted in the expansion of social disconnection. The bombardment of online information in 24-hour news cycles has made us more partisan, less tolerant, and increasingly ignorant about the social world. In our era, political, social, and cultural ignorance is celebrated as we deny the existence of extinction-threatening climate change and champion the wonders of dirty energy production. Such is the perfect storm that helped to set the conditions that enabled Donald Trump to be elected president of the United States. Our love affair with digital technology, according to Sherry Turkle, among many other scholars, has made us less empathetic. In the Age of Trump, are we becoming less social or—worse yet—less human?

I cannot provide a fast and facile answer to this profound question, but can suggest that a more anthropological approach to the world of social life and politics is one way of reclaiming our humanity. I've been doing anthropology for many decades. I've conducted years of research in West Africa and in New York City. I've read widely in the social sciences and in philosophy. During this long and wide-ranging journey, I've made many discoveries. I've also come to terms with my own errors of judgment and interpretation. Having logged many miles on the journey, I've learned that anthropology—at least for me—is a slow social science based not so much on sophisticated analytical frameworks but more on the quality and depth of the social relationships that we have developed over long stretches of time. From this perspective, doing anthropology is, to borrow from my mentor Jean Rouch, a profoundly "shared" practice. A truly shared anthropology foregrounds conversation in face-to-face encounters. Over time those unpredictable and entirely human encounters bring joy as well as sorrow, embarrassment as well as pride, dead ends as well as paths toward greater insight. Shared anthropology is a profound coproduction of knowledge that refines our comprehension of the human condition. It reinforces our shared humanity. If we open our being to others and to the world, we can all practice a shared anthropology.

What are the social and existential rewards of shared anthropology? What happens If we slowly move forward against the grain of fast culture?

The rewards of a slow and shared anthropology are wonderfully underscored in the life work of my colleague and friend, Lisbet Holtedahl, a Norwegian anthropologist and filmmaker who embodies a slow and shared approach to her scholarship and her films. Holtedahl has spent more than 40 years building relationships with people in West Africa—Niger and Cameroon. The intimacy of her shared anthropology is palpable within and between the frames of her films.

In the remarkable film *The Sultan's Burden* (1995), Holtedahl takes us deep into the corridors of Sultan Issa Maigari's palace. From the very first frames, we see the Sultan, who is the spiritual and political leader of the Adamawa Province of Northern Cameroon, walking slowly among his wives, his children, his advisors, and his praise-singers. It is an intimate glimpse—the result of years of shared anthropology—into the character of a proud, traditional leader who is confronting the irrevocable loss of prestige and power as Cameroon begins the process of secular democratization. The film evokes a profoundly human theme: what are the existential dimensions of love and loss?

In her latest film, *Wives*, which was filmed between 1992 and 2015, Holtedahl brings her slow and shared anthropology into the compound of an Islamic scholar, Al Hajji Alkali Ibrahim Goni,who was for 45 years a traditional judge in the aforementioned Sultanate of Issa Maigari. The film showcases the uneven textures of relations between Al Hajji and his many wives, some of whom he divorced, some of whom died, and some of whom he divorced and remarried. In Holtedahl's words, the film describes the "various household scenes of everyday life events and interviews. With this, I hope to identify the audio-visual material's contribution to my understanding of marriage, love and dependency of six of Al Hajji's wives and their husband." At the end of the film Al Hajji Goni, tired and old, is approaching death. From the intimate inside we see how the spread of death's shadow cuts to the core of Al Hajji Goni's humanity and how it changes deep-seated feelings of love and loss in a household so far removed from our experience. In so doing, Holtedahl makes the strange familiar. In so doing, she uses slow and shared anthropology to create emotional and social connections in an increasingly disconnected world.

In the Age of Trump a slow and shared approach to human social relations fosters knowledge in a time of ignorance. It creates webs of social and emotional understanding that transcend our social and cultural differences. By way of edifying conversation, a slow and shared approach to human relations goes a long way toward reclaiming a humanity that fast culture threatens to decimate.

PART THREE

BLOGGING HIGHER EDUCATION: A PUBLIC DEFENSE OF SCHOLARSHIP

INTRODUCTION

Higher education is no stranger to the ravages of fast culture, in which efficient outputs eclipse the slow development of critical thinking and eloquent expression. Indeed, corporate language and ideology have begun the transformation of our colleges and universities into places where students are supposed to acquire "skills" that guarantee a good-paying job. Colleges and universities are fast becoming trade schools that will produce a cadre of unimaginative technocrats. In order to reconstitute the intellectual foundation of our institutions of higher learning, it is important for faculty members to extend the critique of university corporatization. Blogging higher education on public platforms is a potentially powerful way to provide a wide-reaching ground-level critique.

American public higher education is in crisis. As suggested in Part Two of *Adventures in Blogging*, many state legislators believe that public higher education has become a pragmatic vocational pursuit. If they invest in higher education, they argue, there should be good return on investment—a job. They say that subjects like literature, foreign languages, history, philosophy, art, music, sociology, and anthropology, the foundation of a well-rounded liberal education, are "expendable." They suggest that if liberal arts programs cannot guarantee a good job upon graduation, taxpayer dollars should not be allocated to support them. As a consequence, many humanities and social sciences programs at public colleges and universities have been reduced in size or altogether eliminated.

These trends are linked to the corporatization of higher education, in which administrators, whose numbers and salaries are soaring, run universities like businesses. In the corporate university, professors spend exceedingly large amounts of time drafting mission statements; constructing assessment instruments; doing peer, student, and departmental evaluations; and attending training sessions so they can use the latest administrative software, which seems to be updated every six months. There are forms and templates for every imaginable educational activity. Meanwhile reduced intramural and extramural funds for faculty development are increasingly difficult to obtain.

As Maggie Berg and Barbara K. Seeber suggest in their wonderful book *The Slow Professor* (2016), the corporatization of higher education has diverted our attention from the principal missions of colleges and universities: (1) supporting scholarship that enhances our comprehension of the world and (2) training students to think critically and write clearly so they can become engaged and productive citizens. Corporatization, in fact, has created so much tedious "make-work" that professors and students have little time to read, think, or write. Berg and Seeber suggest that professors and students slow down to rediscover the essence of higher education and to reconstitute the fundamental and productive bond that emerges in the relationship of professor to student. In the face of widespread bureaucratization, they also offer common-sense suggestions for recapturing the magic of contemplative and creative higher education.

Writing public blogs about the loss of the university's soul can be an ongoing social media complement to similar critiques in articles, books, and documentary films. Writing this kind of blog is not as time-constrained as doing a news-sensitive contribution on politics. Institutional issues in higher education, after all, have a long history. Many of these issues are fleshed out *ad infinitum* in memos about teaching evaluations, standardization of course syllabi, departmental assessment plans, college, university, and departmental mission statements and five-year plans, and statistics on faculty-student ratios—all of which gives new meaning to the term "productivity."

As should all public posts on social media platforms like *HuffPost*, *Slate*, or *Salon*, higher education blogs should be short and use active voice sentences to make one very strong point. Sometimes short snippets of narrative or references to great literature, like Kafka's *The Castle* (see Chapter 27), can reinforce a point of argument. In higher education blogs, it is often useful to quote bloodless administrative language at length to demonstrate the pervasiveness of the corporate colonization of our colleges and universities.

Blogging higher education from a scholar's standpoint, then, can pressure administrators to rethink their plans for corporatization; it can also bring much needed public attention to these important issues. If a public higher education blog hits the right notes, it might be read ... by ... a very large audience, including local university administrators, and have an impact on the future quality of university life. Because the quality of our educational institutions has a direct bearing on our social and political future, public anthropologists who blog have much to contribute to this important debate.

CHAPTER TWENTY THREE

WINTER BREAK

(DECEMBER 2011)

After what increasingly seems like a lightning fast roller-coaster ride, I recently huffed and puffed my way to submitting final grades, which marked the end my 61st semester of university teaching. You could say that the huffing and puffing is due to my age or my physical condition. Neither would be true. I may be approaching "elder" status, but I am physically fit. You could say that so many years of university teaching have made me weary of the old routines—same subject—anthropology—and the same set of courses. But as time has passed, I've come to enjoy teaching a great deal.

So, if I'm physically fit and enjoy teaching, why do I find myself exhausted by the end of a 15-week semester?

Part of the reason, perhaps, is the importance that our institutions place upon getting grades. Students, of course, have always been very much concerned about grades. Getting good grades has always been a good a way to move forward on the highway that leads to successful careers in medicine, law, information technology, or business. On that venerable highway there has never been much time for taking a frivolous detour that leads to an uncertain destination. In recent years, though, student tunnel vision seems to have become even more narrowly focused. Many of the students I teach would like me to agree to a grand bargain: the best possible grade for the least amount of effort. There are, of course, notable and inspiring exceptions. Even so, every semester students have the chutzpah to ask me to change their grade—for no good reason. Two weeks ago, one of my introductory students who had earned a "C+" wondered if I could change her grade to "B-."

"Can't I get some extra points for attending class?" she asked.

Another student, who had barely passed my introductory class, wrote to me. "Is there any way you could change my grade to a "C-?" she asked, not even offering up her record of attendance as an argument for a grade change.

Fortunately, student encounters about grades, which are always a bit irritating, are few and far between. They don't account for my end-of-semester fatigue.

Something has changed in higher education. When I began professing in 1980, there seemed to be more time to teach. We had the same 15-week semesters, but my courses were much more demanding—for me as well as for my students. We covered more topics and did so in greater depth. The readings were more extensive. I assigned more research papers, which required extensive work in the library. Students found the time come to my office for conversations about anthropology, philosophy, literature, or even the meaning of life! These days most of my students complain about not having enough time to do the course readings, let alone a series of moments to do more than a cursory amount of archival research for a paper. Some of them hand in assignments after the due date. Most of them avoid my office and any kind of serious face-to-face social interaction. Although the aforementioned grade disputes do require some degree of professor-student interaction, they are usually argued in the impersonal domains of cyberspace.

There are external forces that have propelled these educational changes. In these hard times, many contemporary students have to work one or two jobs to pay for college expenses. Accordingly, they have little extra time to read beyond the assignment, daydream, or to take intellectual risks. Contemporary professors, for their part, are so saddled with so many corporately contoured administrative tasks—committee work, assessment studies, assessment workshops, assessment reports, peer evaluations, student evaluations, not to forget large classes to teach, grade, and, lest I forget, assess—that we have little time to think about what we've done or what we want to do.

Every semester overworked students have a limited amount of time to study. Professors are "too busy" to refine their teaching or pursue their research, which usually improves the quality of instruction. Students and professors are trapped in increasingly corporate institutions of higher learning that are designed for processing products—moving student bodies through institutional stages—that produce positive institutional profiles.

Incessant institutional processing produces a great deal of end-of-the-semester student and professorial fatigue, a symptom that something important is missing from the mix of elements on our university campuses. Higher education should be more than a system for processing student bodies. Indeed, it should be the serious attempt to teach young people how to be in the world—an attempt that will set a course for the future.

If we recognize the fatigue for what it is, we should use the Winter Break to recharge our existential batteries and begin anew the pursuit of knowledge.

Here's a New Year's resolution for college students: make a habit of visiting your professors and discussing the world of ideas. Taking such a small step will not only be rewarding for students and professors, but will make the university a little less corporate and a little more humane, which means that everyone benefits.

CHAPTER TWENTY FOUR

WAGING WAR ON HIGHER EDUCATION

(MAY 2012)

Higher education is currently under assault in America. Even in the recent past you could count on bipartisan support of systems of higher education that have long been considered the foundation of American prosperity. We used to think that a robust system of public education was the wellspring of social innovation and scientific invention.

Recent debate in the public sphere, however, has questioned these previously taken for granted assumptions about higher education in America. Indeed, powerful politicians and influential pundits are making suggestions that could undermine higher education, especially public higher education, for years to come.

Consider the views of presumptive GOP presidential candidate Governor Mitt Romney. Given his vantage as one of the super-rich, Mr. Romney seems to be ignorant of the financial hurdles that the vast majority of college and university students must negotiate to get a decent education. Until recently he, like the conservative base of the GOP, supported doubling the interest rates on student loans. As for the loans themselves: no problem.

In an unguarded, unscripted moment he told one student that no one was going to just give her the money she needed. What she needed to do was take advantage of the competitive market and shop around for the best loan rate. In response to another such question, he advised students to find a less expensive college, borrow money from their parents, or start a business.

This kind of Scrooge-like advice is, to put it simply, insulting to the families of the hard-working students that I teach. What's more, these insensitive comments stigmatize public university students. At my university, the students usually don't come from wealthy households in which floating the kids a college or business loan is "no problem." Many of my students work two or sometimes three jobs to support themselves as they take a full load of courses. Because of their financial circumstances, which are, in large measure, shaped by their social class position, they are forced to incur a mounting load of debt from banks interested less in the prospect of their professional future and more in the return on a financial investment. Such an environment is undermining American social mobility and making us even more cynical of rags to riches myths.

In Mr. Romney's view, society—which he often conflates with government—should not make investments in our young people. Young people, Mr. Romney's unguarded comments seem to suggest, should be on their own. Such thinking is a fundamental tenet of GOP and Tea Party orthodoxy.

Mr. Romney's orientation has not only flooded the discourse of talk radio, but has even seeped into the pages of the *New York Times*. In his April 28 "Sunday Review" column, "The Imperiled Promise of College," *NYT* columnist Frank Bruni ponders the "usefulness" of undergraduate education. Citing Associated Press data of 2011, he laments the "fact" that

> 53.6 percent of college graduates under the age of 25 were unemployed, or, if they were lucky, merely underemployed, which means they were in jobs for which their degrees weren't necessary. Philosophy majors mull questions no more existential than the proper billowiness of the foamed milk atop a customer's cappuccino. Anthropology majors contemplate the tribal behavior of the youngsters who shop at Zara where they peddle skinny jeans.

Beyond the demonstration of his ignorance of things philosophical or anthropological, Mr. Bruni's somewhat sneering attitude toward anthropology, philosophy, zoology, art history, and all of the humanities unveils an anti-intellectual utilitarianism that is far more sinister than Mr. Romney's awkward insensitivity to economic struggle.

Mr. Bruni seems to suggest that you should go to college to acquire job skills that will give you a competitive edge in an increasingly skill-focused job market. In short, he is suggesting that we use student aid, if such a thing would exist in a Romney administration, to push students toward math and science education. There's nothing wrong with that idea. Math and science students deserve our support. But does that mean that we should abandon the study of philosophy, the history of art, or the analysis of society and culture?

Is public higher education a place for skill acquisition or is it space for teaching young people how to think? If we move toward the former—following the short-sighted lead of politicians like Rick Scott or Mitt Romney or perhaps the ideas of pundits like Frank Bruni—we will produce a highly skilled population of workers who, like automatons, will follow a complex set of instructions, but won't know how to connect those instructions to a broader technological or social context. By contrast, if we train young people in creative thinking, which, by the way, is not limited to humanities and social sciences, we will produce educated citizens who will know how to think, innovate, and invent. Without such a fundamental long-term investment, our anachronistic and unimaginative economy will continue to fade away, which means there will be few, if any, jobs for anyone.

CHAPTER TWENTY FIVE

HIGHER EDUCATION'S TRAIN TO NOWHERE

(SEPTEMBER 2013)

There is an alarming disconnect in contemporary higher education. As I have been saying in this space for more than two years, the university-as-corporation threatens to undermine the foundation of a world-class system of education and diminish the quality of our future social life.

One of the ramifications of university corporatization has been an increasing disregard for the intellectual dimensions of the professorial life. In the name of technological efficiency, an increasingly bloated cadre of university technocrats flood our in-boxes with mindless minutiae. These institutional requirements—assessment outcomes, mission statements, five-year plans, and so on—have become so burdensome that there is precious little time for intellectual pursuit. During the academic year, it is difficult to find the "leisure" to read current research reports, prepare grant proposals, design new courses, refine lectures, or write an article or a book. In the current environment of institutional reviews and performance assessments, who has time to think?

From my vantage of being in the university teaching trenches for more than 30 years, I have witnessed the slow but inexorable erosion of respect for professors. The once-valued life of the mind is increasingly seen as flighty, anachronistic or, worse yet, counter-productive. There is a widespread belief—even among university technocrats—that professors get paid a great deal for very little work. A comment on one of my blogs, "Back to the Struggle Against Ignorance," is a case in point: "Are there any professors left in this country who actually teach and do research, or are they all on the public dole so they can write blogs for the *Huffington Post?*"

If you think my suggestion is a tad overblown, consider how the administrative technocrats at the University of Oregon (UO) are trying to limit the "privacy" of a world-class faculty. As part of the negotiation of a first contract between a new faculty union and the UO administration, UO expressed its desire to monitor the emails of faculty members. Here is the language of a UO counter-proposal dated 8/29/13, "Article 49: Acceptable Use of University Information Assets." It was published on the University of Oregon website.

> Bargaining unit faculty members have no expectation of privacy in emails, files, documents, or other information created or stored on university information assets. The university may monitor the use of, and review documents and other information stored on university information assets. Emails sent on a bargaining unit faculty member's non-university email account and information created or stored on non-university computer systems belong to the bargaining unit member except to the extent that they address work-related subjects.

The aim of this policy may well be to "rein in" faculty opinion—even those expressed in private email accounts if they concern work-related subjects. Since many, if not most, professors work at home and write a wide variety of messages that are "work-related," the UO administration looks like it wants to cast a wide net of surveillance over faculty communications—especially, I would suppose, those that are critical of university personnel or policies.

The broader implication of this policy smacks of university corporatization. Looking for incidences of personal abuse, corporations routinely monitor the emails of employees. In the same manner, the

UO administration wants to ensure faculty "informational asset compliance." The intent of such a proposed policy is insulting, an example of the erosion of institutional respect for university and college professors.

It is equally insulting to see how much money floods into the administrative coffers on our campuses. Consider the administrative bloat at Purdue University that John Hechinger described last year in *Bloomberg News*. He quoted J. Paul Robinson, president of Purdue's Faculty Senate, as he walked by his university's administrative tower:

> "I have no idea what these people do," said Robinson, waving his hand across a row of offices, his voice rising.
>
> The 59-year-old professor of biomedical engineering is leading a faculty revolt against bureaucratic bloat at the public university in Indiana. In the past decade, the number of administrative employees jumped 54 percent, almost eight times the growth of tenured and tenure-track faculty.
>
> Purdue has a $313,000-a-year acting provost and six vice and associate vice provosts, including a $198,000 chief diversity officer. It employs 16 deans and 11 vice presidents, among them a $253,000 marketing officer and a $433,000 business school chief...
>
> "We're a public university," Robinson said. "We're here to deliver a high-quality education at as low a price as possible. Why is it that we can't find any money for more faculty, but there seems to be an almost unlimited budget for administrators?"

There is administrative bloat at the public university where I teach—lots of vice presidents, associate vice presidents, assistant vice presidents, program directors, associate provosts, and associate deans. These administrators, of course, need support staff. The ever-growing cadre of administrators and staff, of course, requires office space. Amid a campus-building boom—new dormitories, a world-class fitness center, and new parking lots—there is an ironic shortage of instructional space, which means that students are crowded into old stuffy classrooms. Given the aforementioned expansion of staff, there is also a shortage of office space, which means that new faculty members are often forced to "double up" in substandard spaces. Meanwhile, we are bombarded with administrative pabulum. Do our syllabi conform to the university template? Have we used the correct terms in our mission statements? Have we adhered to a huge assortment of university guidelines? Have we met our student processing goals?

Granted, universities are large institutions with extensive budgets and challenging institutional issues. We need administrators to run our institutions of higher education. But universities are not corporations. In a September 8 blog published in the English-language version of *Al Jazeera*, Santiago Zabala, a philosopher at the University of Barcelona, cut through the technocratic balderdash to focus on the heart of the matter:

> For those of us who had the good fortune to be educated by teachers who guided our intellectual interest and social wellbeing regardless of where we were enrolled, we know it's always the faculty that makes the difference, not the institution. If, as Noam Chomsky once pointed out, "our kids are being prepared for passive obedience, not creative, independent lives," it's because we live in a corporate world where most institutions are ranked according to criteria that too often ignore the essence of the discipline in favour of the job market.

Professor Zabala went on to write:

> In other words, colleges and universities are actively undermining one of their basic tenets—to educate and equip a citizenry to make society a better place, in great part by challenging unjust and abusive power. When you combine this unreflective and shallow environment with the corporate takeover of the academy, you turn the education process into a means to make more and more profit. A profit mentality driving the educational environment will necessarily ignore building a conscious community that is intentional about learning, and serious about forming citizens who can

think critically and question society. To do that, learning environments must be intentionally formed so that students can learn to focus on serious and sustained reflection.

The technocratic elites who run our universities are not likely to seriously consider Professor Zabala's argument—too pie in the sky, too "counterproductive." Most of them have already boarded a train en route to the innovative, market-savvy, and technologically sophisticated future of higher education. What they tend to overlook, however, is that without a strong, creative, well-supported, and well-respected faculty, they are riding on a train to nowhere.

CHAPTER TWENTY SIX

A 2014 CHALLENGE FOR THE SOCIAL SCIENCES

(JANUARY 2014)

The beginning of a new year always compels professional reflection. As I head back into the classroom to face a new set of students— some eager, some not so eager—one gripping realization colonizes my thoughts: social scientists are living in increasingly challenging times. It is now commonplace to read reports about the demise of the liberal arts, including, of course, the social sciences. In states like North Carolina, once the very model of excellence in public higher education, there is a politically driven movement to dump the "irrelevant" and "unproductive" social sciences and humanities into the academic dustbin. Last year North Carolina Governor Pat McCrory wondered if public funds—taxpayers' dollars—should be used to fund "unproductive" disciplines like philosophy. Here's an exchange he had with conservative stalwart William Bennett, which is summarized in Kevin Kiley's *Inside Higher Education* article, "Another Liberal Arts Critic":

> "How many Ph.Ds. in philosophy do I need to subsidize?" Bennett asked, to which McCrory replied, "You and I agree." (Bennett earned a Ph.D. from a public flagship university, the University of Texas at Austin, in philosophy.)

McCrory's comments on higher education echo statements made by a number of Republican governors—including those in Texas, Florida, and Wisconsin—who have questioned the value of liberal arts instruction and humanities degrees at public colleges and universities. Those criticisms have started to coalesce into a potential Republican agenda on higher education, emphasizing reduced state funding, low tuition prices, vocational training, performance funding for faculty members, state funding tied to job placement in "high demand" fields, and taking on flagship institutions.

Does such a movement suggest the erosion of education in the liberal arts at public institutions of higher learning? In previous blogs, I have repeatedly described how the politicization and corporatization of universities is eroding intellectual quality. Universities have become institutions that increasingly measure excellence by the number of students processed rather than by the capacity of graduates to think critically and write clearly.

In this rather repressive intellectual climate, what can be done to salvage the liberal arts? Beyond very necessary grassroots movements of students, faculty, and parents to protest the politicization—and slow deaths—of world-class public institutions of higher learning, there are a number of things that professors can do to enhance the public profile of the liberal arts, giving them a measure of social and political potency.

The challenge for the social sciences—at least for me—is to simultaneously maintain rigorous standards while producing works that clearly and powerfully articulate important insights to broad audiences across a variety of media. In my discipline, anthropology, the challenge is to communicate critical insights about social life in such a way that moves audiences to think and to act.

Many of my colleagues devote considerable energy to debate the whys and wherefores of nature, culture, social change, globalization, and ontological turns. These debates are usually articulated in specialized languages that may demonstrate brilliance but often limit the reach of insight. There is no reason that theoretically informed findings cannot be communicated to broad audiences.

I present two recent examples from authors who are anthropologists. The first is David Graeber's book *Debt: The First 5,000 Years*.

Although the multidimensional subject of debt can be frustratingly complex, Graeber presents his anthropologically informed ideas in a conversational manner, which means he is able to transform a complex tangle of information, some of which is highly abstract, into a readable history of how the notion of debt has shaped economic, social, religious, and political relations. The upshot is that this highly sophisticated but accessible work is beginning to change the way we think about something fundamentally human. Such an impact has broad implications for the future of our social, economic, and political relations. In short, *Debt* is a book that is both academically rigorous and broadly appealing. It showcases the power and the reach of the social sciences.

The second example is Alisse Waterston's *My Father's Wars: Migration, Memory, and the Violence of a Century*, which is an anthropologically and historically informed memoir on the impact of social upheaval on the social, economic, and emotional life of one man, Michael Waterston, who fled Poland, landed in Cuba, and eventually made his way to New York City. Waterston writes:

> This is a story that is also a history.... It is a portrait of a charming, funny, wounded, and difficult man, his relationships with those he loved, and his most sacred beliefs. And it is a reflection on the forces of history, the power of memory, and meanings people attach to events, things and others.

In this book, Waterston employs the considerable power of narrative—a daughter's intimate but thoroughly anthropological account of her father's fascinatingly troubled life—to connect with her readers. In so doing she demonstrates how powerful historical forces have a tangible impact on the everyday dramas of family life. Such a tack gives her book broad appeal. Although *Debt* and *My Father's Wars* are very different kinds of books, they share one important feature: they both demonstrate quite palpably how the forces of history or of debt—abstract forces—have a real impact on our everyday lives. These are works that engage the public. They are works that compel readers to think, feel, and act.

The public advocacy of anthropology's founding father, Franz Boas, long ago set the standard for social scientific public engagement. He expended his considerable academic capital on a long battle against racism and social intolerance. As a 2014 challenge, it is perhaps time for more social scientists to follow his lead in order to demonstrate the indispensability of the social sciences. Our future depends upon it.

CHAPTER TWENTY SEVEN

KAFKA ON CAMPUS

(MARCH 2014)

College campuses are fast becoming strange places where nothing makes much sense, where everything creates a haze of confusion and dislocation, where, to quote an idiom from the Songhay people of Niger and Mali, "you don't know your front side from your backside." Such a state makes me feel much like "K," the protagonist of *The Castle*, which is arguably Kafka's greatest novel, a narrative of palpably disturbed dislocation and social alienation.

Writing about Kafka's great work in the *Guardian* in late December 2011, William Burrows suggests that it is a common mistake to think that *The Castle* is fundamentally a critique of mindless bureaucracy. Instead he suggests that

> Kafka writes about simple and important things: aloneness, pain, the longing for human companionship, the need to be respected and understood, sex, and the struggle of being employed ... This book will make you sad for the things missing in your life. The reader is forced into confrontation with basic human need. We bear witness to K's futile

struggle for recognition and respect. The whole ground of his being is undermined by those who will not acknowledge his task or his right to be in the village.

For me, the corporate university has become Kafka's Castle. In our struggle for "recognition and respect," students and faculty have become much like Kafka's character "K." Although we are an integral part of the academy, we feel left out—numb. The reason for our sad state of disorientation is that the university has become a corporation that provides "services." As such, the corporate university must ceaselessly produce protocols and mind-boggling procedures that measure the "quality" of its "product." In this product-oriented atmosphere of service provision, we wander about Kafka's Campus in states of disorientation.

What can we expect?

How can we proceed?

Overwhelmed by incessant emails, policy changes, assessment exercises, learning outcomes, and mission statements, we don't know where to turn in our search for an education or a meaningful life. Some readers may think I'm exaggerating the sad state of contemporary higher education. I wish that were so.

Consider a recent ad that appeared in *Higher Ed Jobs* for an assistant professorship of English at Texas A&M – Kingsville. In bold face letters, the ad states a requirement for the job: "Provide Excellent Customer Service."

In his recent blog "How Did We Get Into This Mess?" Professor David Perry stated:

> I do not provide service to my students. When I am at my best, and let's face it, I am not always at my best, I drive my students, encourage them, plead, cajole, debate, critique, and praise them. This is not service. And importantly, while our relationship is enmeshed in broad systems of exchange, we are not in an exchange-based relationship.
>
> ...Students are not my customers and thank goodness for that, because the responsibility of a teacher to his or her students is far greater than the employee to the customer.

One of the most important features of customer service is assessment—of employees and products. Indeed, the university-as-corporation is awash in assessment—so much so that it is hard to make your way as a student or a professor. Consider the Kafkaesque document that the assessors at my institution, who spend much of their time in The Castle, sent to faculty members. Titled "Assessment of Student Learning Outcomes Within Academic Programs at ...," this missive identifies key terms (academic units as opposed to professional education units, assessment reports, TracDat Assessment Tracking software, TracDat Periodic Updates, and reporting groups that "are responsible for implementing and overseeing the assessment process for individual programs and/or departments").

The document lists seven hyperlinks that explain who gets assessed, what an assessment plan looks like, who coordinates the reporting of student learning outcomes, how assessment results might be applied, the assessment time line, where the assessment results might be published as well as the institutional resources that support the assessment of student learning. If someone is interested in writing about assessment results, he or she

> must include, at minimum, a listing of all programmatic student learning outcomes, but could also include
>
> 1. examples of the specific skills students are expected to acquire as a result of the experiences within a curricular program;
> 2. types of knowledge and/or dispositions that students in a particular program are expected to demonstrate or develop with regard to each general programmatic student learning outcome.

It goes without saying that "course learning objectives and programmatic student learning outcome information must be included on all course syllabi. Furthermore, the course learning objectives must be linked, directly, to programmatic student learning outcomes."

Such a range of assessment requirements is enough to steer students into a bank of thick fog. Such stuff will certainly make any professor's head spin. Having labored for more than 30 years in university classrooms, I have a few simple questions to ask the people who work in The Castle.

1. Do you really think students, professors, or the public will read and discuss the highly manicured and thoroughly debated course learning outcomes, let alone programmatic student learning outcomes? In an era during which people don't read very much, they're not likely to savor this kind of dull bureaucratic prose.

2. Do you really think you can use quantitative means to "measure" things like critical thinking, clarity of expression, or creativity? In my experience, it is a mistake to reduce the human condition to a set of outcomes.

Like most undergraduates, my students are preoccupied with exams, research papers, and, dare I say it, grades. They don't give a damn about student learning outcomes. The same can be said for most professors who don't want to waste their time writing mission statements, student learning outcomes, and assessment reports. Wouldn't it be better if we devoted more of our time to refining our knowledge, reworking our class presentations, or writing essays and books—all of which enable us to inspire our students, all of which enable us to introduce our students to the complex wonders of the world?

If I were to assess the assessors, I would make two suggestions. First, I would urge you to leave The Castle. If you manage to find your way out, why not explore the open spaces of the classroom? Try teaching a course, which is a good way to recognize and respect the students and professors you are bent on assessing. Second, I would recommend that you read—or reread—*The Castle*, to get an intense sense of the existential consequences of transforming universities into customer service institutions.

CHAPTER TWENTY EIGHT

THE BRAVE NEW WORLD OF CAMPUS LIFE

(APRIL 2014)

The American Association of University Professors (AAUP) recently released a report that compares faculty and administrator compensation. It comes as no surprise that the salaries of administrators and coaches, according to the AAUP report, have skyrocketed. Meanwhile, faculty salaries, which inched forward for the first time in five years, continue to lag. The authors of the report also discussed trends in academic spending and found that colleges and universities are spending less and less on instruction and more and more on athletics. In her *Washington Post* article on the AAUP report, Jena McGregor quoted Saranna Thornton, an economics professor and chair of AAUP's Committee on the Economic Status of the Profession:

> "The biggest takeaway is that the education mission of institutions is becoming less and less important," Thompson says. Athletics and administrative functions are getting increasing shares of the budget, she says. In some cases, that's understandable, due to necessary costs that have grown inherently over time, such as technology spending. But in other cases it's driven by universities' efforts to make their campuses more attractive as competition for students grows.

"One of the myths that we want to explode," Thornton
says, "is that it's faculty salaries that are driving the increase
in higher education."

The AAUP report is yet another indication of a cultural shift in the
American university. If the numbers in the AAUP report are indicative, we now live in an era in which the educational mission of our
colleges and universities has become marginal. Given the marginal-
ization of the educational mission, can we still refer to our colleges
and universities as "institutions of higher learning"?

If you follow the money, you get a pretty good picture of the cultural logic that is streaming through contemporary American universities. This logic has created a universe in which the deep scholarship
of the academy takes a back seat to the superficial window dressing
of marketing slogans. In such a universe, capital improvement projects and athletics receive more funding that does instruction. In this
emerging atmosphere administrators run "operations," students are
"consumers," and faculty become "employees." As an employee, a
professor's contribution to scholarship, which is sometimes difficult
to measure, becomes less important than his or her "productivity"—
the number of students processed each semester, the number of students he or she guides through the graduation portal. If performance
objectives are met, you might get a slight raise in salary or your academic department's annual budget might even get a slight increase,
though this happy outcome is far from guaranteed in the cold world
of cost-benefit analysis.

In the corporate university, of course, employees must look
after their customers, making sure that they are satisfied with the
"product," making sure that they have enough "credit" to graduate.
Indeed, campaigns of customer satisfaction have reduced academic
standards and promoted widespread grade inflation. Commenting on
this phenomenon in the April 4–6 edition of *CounterPunch*, Anthony
Dimaggio wrote:

Consider some of the recent evidence for the decline in
academic standards. In the early 1960s, full-time college students spent 40 hours per week on their academic

activities—including class attendance, homework, studying, and writing. By the 2000s, the number had declined
to 27 hours for full-time students—a reduction of 33 percent. Similarly, the time spent studying decreased from
25 hours in 1961 to 13 hours in 2003, a reduction of nearly
50 percent. Today, many students expect classes with little reading, as a third of social science students who are
surveyed avoid classes with more than 40 pages of reading
per week.

The decline of standards is accompanied by incredible grade
inflation. Recent research on American grades found that a massive
easing of standards took place across hundreds of colleges and universities in the last 50 years. About 15% of all grades were "A"s in
the 1940s and 1950s, while about a third of grades were "B"s, a third
were "C"s, and about 20% were "D"s or "F"s. By the late 2000s, the
percentage of "A"s was nearly 45%, "B"s were 30%, and "Cs" were
15%. Just 10% of grades were "D"s or "F"s.
Even if university "employees" are dedicated to consumer satisfaction, their bosses need to be certain that they are putting forth their
best efforts. The consumers are regularly surveyed about their classroom experience. Consumer "outcomes" are measured and assessed.
Employees must also be monitored. Is the content of their courses
beyond the boundary of "consumer" acceptability? As "representatives
of the university," do professors need to "censor" that content? What
if professors say or write something that is not consumer-friendly?
What's more, if professorial behavior is not institution-friendly, what
can be done—reprimand, early retirement (as was the ploy with the
University of Colorado's Professor Patti Adler), suspension, or out-
right dismissal? At the University of Oregon, administrators sought
the power to monitor professors' correspondence both on and off
campus. The Kansas Board of Regents wanted to be able to fire any
public university professor who said or wrote something that was not
in the "interest" of the university.
What are the social ramifications of this Brave New World of
Campus Life? Consider once again the commentary of Anthony
Dimaggio:

In his new book, *Neoliberalism's War on Higher Education*, Henry Giroux insightfully warns Americans about an educational system that promotes a "culture of idiocy and illiteracy" that's fueled in large part by the "corporatization of the university." Colleges and universities, Giroux explains, foster "a mode of public pedagogy that privileges the entrepreneurial subject while encouraging a value system that promotes self-interest, if not an unchecked selfishness." Giroux's attacks on higher education will be met by nods among those fighting on the frontlines against efforts to lobotomize college classrooms and transform campuses into vocational facilities that pump out new units (a.k.a. "graduates").

There are an increasing number of scholars who, like Giroux, stand strongly against the corporate university. Like Giroux, we decry the demise of academic standards and are troubled by the emerging culture of ignorance. We realize that in the age of social media and the "inviolability" of the market, much about the university has changed. Even so, it is important to defend scholarship and our mission as educators. As we struggle against the stiff headwinds of corporatization, the lack of progress can make us weary. No matter the depth of our weariness we need to remain steadfast and remember that in time prevailing winds do change direction.

CHAPTER TWENTY NINE

MAGICAL MENTORS

(MAY 2014)

It's once again graduation time on our nation's college and university campuses. Streams of notables, including President Obama and First Lady Michelle Obama, have or will soon be trickling over ceremonial spaces to speak to the graduates—about boundless opportunity.

Commencement speeches are, after all, about fresh beginnings. Some speakers may also talk about the challenges of higher education, the dangers lurking in the world, or about the prospect of living in changing climates that promise ongoing droughts, persistent heat waves, stronger blizzards, powerful tornadoes, and destructive hurricanes. Most commencement speakers, though, are likely to discuss platitudinous themes that are designed for important rites of passage. The proud graduates, after all, are to be ceremonially transformed from students into adults. The pomp and circumstance, which is likely to translate into routinely uninspiring events, often avoid mention of important life issues that are central to how a graduate's life might develop.

Graduation always makes me think about importance of mentors in a person's life. Indeed, universities are trying to make mentoring more central to their missions. Universities have mentoring programs and mentoring training. At my university, there is a worthy program in which senior scholars mentor their junior colleagues. There was a National Mentoring Summit held in January of this year. In October, the University of New Mexico's Mentoring Institute will host its annual conference for which the keynote is titled "The Dynamics of Coaching and Mentoring Relationships in the Workplace." The conference will also feature workshops on how to inspire student creativity, how to design effective mentoring programs, and how to engage the power of positive mentoring.

Survey data seem to underscore the power of positive mentoring. In the May 2006 issue of the *Chronicle of Higher Education*, Scott Carlson wrote:

> If you believe the new "Gallup-Purdue Index Report," a study of 30,000 graduates of American colleges on issues of employment, job engagement, and well-being, it all comes down to old-fashioned values and human connectedness. One of the report's big takeaways: College graduates, whether they went to a hoity-toity private college or a mid-tier public, had double the chances of being engaged in their work and were three times as likely to be thriving in their well-being if they connected with a professor on the campus who stimulated them, cared about them, and encouraged their hopes and dreams.
>
> College graduates had double the odds of being engaged at work and three times the odds of thriving in Gallup's five elements of well-being if they had had "emotional support"—professors who "made me excited about learning," "cared about me as a person," or "encouraged my hopes and dreams."

It's clear that mentoring skills are important, but I wonder if the answer to mentoring issues lies in institutes and programs? Many people may feel mentoring is beside the point. Given the privations of the corporate university, others may be too busy filling out forms or completing assessment exercises to mentor their students or junior colleagues. Some folks just might not have the "right stuff" to mentor successfully. Sometimes the most powerful mentor-mentee relationships "happen" as two wandering life paths unexpectedly cross.

My development as a scholar and human being devolves in large measure from lessons learned from two mentors I stumbled upon in West Africa—the late filmmaker, Jean Rouch, and the late Songhay healer-philosopher, Adamu Jenitongo. In both cases our master-apprentice relationship was not based upon a program or on coaching techniques, but on mutual respect and love. It was also a relationship premised upon the mutual acknowledgment that the mentor was all-knowing and that the mentee knew little, if anything at all—a difficult pill for this author and for most people to swallow.

My mentors never told me what to do. They taught by way of example. They led their lives and did their work, allowing me to watch them perform their magic-in-the-world. At the right moment, they took my hand and led me into their world, but they eventually pointed me in a direction and let go so I could find my own way. They expected nothing in return.

They also adhered to a West African theory of learning. When you are young, you listen and watch your elders. When they decide that you have made progress in your specialization (weaving, fishing, farming, music, poetry, the arts, science, or social science), they gently push you onto the path of mastery. In time, you put into practice what you have learned, and your work helps to make the world a better place. By the time you become an elder, you confront your greatest obligation—to pass your knowledge on to the next generation—a true mentor, someone to guide you in a fruitful direction that leads to well-being-in-the world.

It takes hard work to engage the power of the mentor-mentee relationship. Even so, the existential rewards of such contact last a lifetime. If you are a graduate and haven't had a mentor, find one in your next stage of life. If you can be a mentor, take several mentees under your wing and encourage them to follow their dreams.

Mentorship is magical. It can be the difference that makes a difference. It can be the tonic that sweetens life-in-the-world.

CHAPTER THIRTY

WE'RE NUMBER ONE

(AUGUST 2014)

Every year business-oriented publications like *Forbes*, the *Wall Street Journal*, and *Kiplinger's* rate college majors. What are the best and worst courses of study for getting a good, well-paying job after graduation? It's hardly surprising that disciplines in the social sciences and humanities rank much lower than engineering and information technology. In the latest twist to the ranking game, H&R Block analysts have compared and contrasted postgraduate unemployment rates.

In her June 5 piece in *HuffPost*, Emily Thomas summarized the H&R Block infographic:

> According to the chart, recent graduates who majored in social sciences and creative fields like anthropology, film, fine arts and graphic design faced the biggest unemployment rates (about 10–12 percent). Conversely, the top industries for recent graduates were found to be advertising, followed by computer software and finance.

Even though anthropology is not a "creative field," it is nonetheless at the very top of the H&R Block chart of worst college majors. Based on the rankings of *Kiplinger's*, the *Wall Street Journal*, and H&R Block as well as the statements of Florida Governor Rick Scott (whose daughter, lest we forget, was an anthropology major) and other believers in the infallibility of the "market," you have to be a fool to major in disciplines like anthropology, foreign languages, philosophy, film-video, or, worse yet, "liberal arts." From the vantage of this mentality, these disciplines may promise intellectual stimulation or even some degree of passion, but offer little return on your investment dollar.

These rankings are sadly similar to President Obama's proposal to create a university ranking system based upon graduate and postgraduate employment rates and salary levels. As Jamienne Studley, one of President Obama's education officials, put it: "ranking a university is as easy as rating a blender. Go to a university with a good four-year graduation rate and pick a major that will ensure good postgraduate job placement."

This business-model product evaluation discourse, it seems, has slithered its way through multiple levels of college and university administrations and has now emerged at the highest levels of the federal government. Given its pervasive power, the corporate university model threatens to transform our institutions of higher education from arenas of intellectual pursuit to job training centers. No need for extraneous thinking or pondering the whys and wherefores of life. Just master the essentials, get certified, and move out into the "real world."

Such a pragmatic vision has many advocates among university administrators and state and federal officials. Their zeal for the university-as-blender model has triggered higher education budget cuts and the reduction or elimination of "non-productive" programs like foreign languages, art history, and philosophy. Even so, there is growing concern among some members of the business community that our soon-to-be factories of higher education will spit out an ever-expanding cadre of narrowly focused, mindless, and clueless automatons.

In his insightful *Inside Higher Education* article "Business and The Liberal Arts," published in 2013, the former CEO of the Seagram Corporation, Edgar M. Bronfman, wrote about the value of a liberal arts degree:

My advice, however, is simple, but well-considered: Get a liberal arts degree. In my experience, a liberal arts degree is the most important factor in forming individuals into interesting and interested people who can determine their own paths through the future.

For all of the decisions young business leaders will be asked to make based on facts and figures, needs and wants, numbers and speculation, all of those choices will require one common skill: how to evaluate raw information, be it from people or a spreadsheet, and make reasoned and critical decisions. The ability to think clearly and critically—to understand what people mean rather than what they say—cannot be monetized, and in life should not be undervalued. In all the people who have worked for me over the years the ones who stood out the most were the people who were able to see beyond the facts and figures before them and understand what they mean in a larger context.

I am sometimes shocked when I encounter students, often graduating seniors, who don't know how to use the library. Many of these students have never conducted archival research. Many of them have never organized and written a research paper. Instead they tend to take multiple-choice exams and learn "what's needed" so they can pass the test.

If you major in anthropology or just about any other social science or humanity, it's very likely that you'll leave the university as a broadly educated person. Chances are you will have developed the analytical skills to evaluate a set of data, interpret those data, and then, based upon those interpretations, make critical judgments. These moves are the very essence of what Mr. Bronfman calls "the ability to think clearly and critically." By the time most of my students earn their undergraduate degrees in anthropology, they have the capacity to "to understand what people mean rather than what they say." Indeed, as scholars of social life and culture, my anthropology students know how to place events in larger social, political, and economic contexts.

The value of these analytical and expository skills is hard to quantify and difficult to rank. They certainly cannot be compared and contrasted like blenders or vacuum cleaners. As educators, it is our obligation to teach the aforementioned skills to our students, skills that will make them more thoughtful and productive participants in the workforce, skills that will make them better citizens, skills that will ensure a future of innovation and invention.

For me, that's a record that corresponds to a real number one designation.

CHAPTER THIRTY ONE

A LETTER FROM THE UNDERGROUND
OF THE CASTLE

(SEPTEMBER 2014)

Dear Friends and Colleagues:

As another academic year begins, *The Castle*'s shadow is bringing more and more Kafkaesque darkness to university campuses. That shadow continues to transform our places of higher learning into corporate enclaves in which mindless civility eclipses uncomfortable debate, in which bureaucratic process becomes more important than creative discovery, in which business professionals, who know little about the life of the mind, make decisions that adversely impact the quality of campus intellectual life.

The increasing length of The Castle's shadow makes me sad; it compels me to seek the solace and protection of The Underground. Like most professors these days, I need some protection. As an increasingly inconsequential faculty member at a public university, a person who enjoys teaching, who feels obligated to challenge the minds of his students, I feel despondent as I try to extricate myself from a flurry of bureaucratic obligations that take precious time away from what should be the primary mission of higher education: quality teaching informed by cutting edge knowledge of disciplinary research. It takes time to conduct research, write scholarly papers, and prepare course materials, all the while making sure that you're up to date in your discipline. And yet, those pursuits seem insignificant in the dim shadow of The Castle.

The men and women who spend their days in The Castle see the university from a different perspective. It is a perspective that doesn't connect with the realities of the classroom or with the twists and turns of intellectual life. If this disconnect continues, our universities will be transformed into training schools in which graduates are not taught how to think, but how to be obedient workers who don't question authority. In an America that has become economically polarized, this educational strategy fits the plans and dreams of a new legion of oligarchs, who usually prefer blind loyalty to perceptive critique.

From my vantage in The Castle's Underground, it is clear that the people who reside in The Castle do not trust professors to do their jobs. In the corporate university, we (professors) have to show them (administrators, boards of trustees, and legislators) numbers that prove that our "product"—teaching course x or y—effectively meets their projected goals.

This lack of trust translates into pervasive assessment. For most of us in the professoriate, the scourge of university assessment is a monumental vote of no confidence in our professional capacities. Assessment exercises keep the ever-expanding number of administrators quite busy. They spend a lot of their time processing ever-increasing amounts of data, the production of which is soaking up more and more of our attention. That means that we have less time to do our work. As for the students, they usually care about workloads and grades and don't give a hoot about learning outcomes and assessment data.

This destructive madness is widespread on our campuses. Here is an example from my university, which, when it comes to assessment, is not at all exceptional. Consider what the residents of Our Castle, who have never visited my classroom, expect of the professors in my department—an "Action Plan." Here's the short version.

1. Revise assessment plans for consistency with clear rationales for determination of student success;

2. Upload all assessment plans to TracDat, a mysterious data cloud somewhere in cyberspace;
3. Use assessment to improve programs;
4. Make sure our assessment is consistent with general education assessment requirements;
5. Correct syllabi to be consistent with university requirements;
6. Assess and improve distance education offerings and share distance education experience with the campus;
7. Encourage faculty proficiency in classroom technology; and
8. Make sure syllabi contain required elements.

This "Action Plan" will produce a data set that will be uploaded to the mysterious TracDat, where faceless people in The Castle will evaluate and reevaluate our work. How useful will these data sets be? Can you measure student success any more than you can measure happiness or well-being? Can assessment improve programs or instruction if professors don't have adequate time to pursue their scholarship? Why is consistency so institutionally important? Is consistency more important that the quality of course content? Does technological proficiency, which is, of course, important, guarantee teaching excellence and student success? If you look at the boilerplate of assessment, you find little in it about taking time to refine scholarship, or engage in research-informed teaching. There is little or no mention of faculty keeping up with disciplinary developments. Between the bloodless lines of Castle boilerplate, however, there are bullet points about templates, consistency, outcomes, and strategic plans.

When I occasionally emerge from The Underground and look up at The Castle, I sometimes feel numb. After more than 30 years in the classroom, I wonder about The Castle's increasing insistence that we engage in pointless make-work that diverts our attention from our professional obligations. It makes no sense at all.

Do people in The Castle desire professional mediocrity?

It's hard to know. The people in The Castle don't talk to us. They don't seem to like us very much, let alone trust us to do our jobs. They don't seem to pay very much attention to scholarly achievements that bring recognition and prestige to the university. They do seem to like technology and distance education—"innovation" that cuts costs and increases revenue. At my university, there's a lot of easy money to develop distance education and hybrid courses. There seems to be less money for highly competitive faculty research grants.

The people in The Castle like numbers, outcomes, and action plans—things that tend to alienate those of us who seek intellectual refuge in The Underground. When will the isolated figures up in The Castle come out into the dim light they have created and realize that people are more important than processes, that support and respect for scholarship goes a long way toward restoring faculty morale, which, in turn, would improve teaching effectiveness and student success?

The residents of The Castle, however, seem to be true believers in the corporate university. Given their track record, they are not likely to soon understand how destructive their actions have been to the mission of higher education. Higher education certainly needs to better incorporate technology into university teaching, but if that change diminishes scholarship or subverts faculty innovation, invention, and creativity, what's left?

Some critics might suggest that if professors are not happy with their lives in the corporate university, they should leave—find another job or retire. That's the easy way out. Despite the hardships, world-class face-to-face teaching still occurs down here in The Underground of The Castle. Down here we invest in people more than in things. Down here we try and sometimes succeed in inspiring some of our students. When that happens, our dark corridors are suddenly illuminated with light—real student success.

PART FOUR

BLOGGING MEDIA IN THE ERA OF FAST NEWS

INTRODUCTION

In fast culture, slow journalism is hard to find. Even foreign correspondents sometimes lack basic knowledge of the countries on which they report. I'll never forget meeting a woman who was soon heading off to Africa as a *New York Times* foreign correspondent. Having never studied things African or visited an African nation, she wanted advice about living conditions, language use, politics, and history. Her lack of knowledge shocked me. I had naively thought that the *New York Times* would send someone to Africa with at least a degree of specialized knowledge.

When it comes to contemporary media representation, there is much for public scholars to critique. In the US, pundits who pontificate on television and radio are often ignorant of the nuances of social life, social class, or, for that matter, the fine points of policy. In 2016, they gave too much media time to people like Donald Trump who deftly used the media's thirst for good ratings to spread conspiracy theories—the foundation of an "alternate reality," the power of which helped to propel Trump all the way to the White House. Now that Trump is president of the United States, the media are compelled to give him a platform for an endless series of misrepresentations—a nice way of saying lies—about the size of his electoral victory, the extent of his inauguration crowds, the "massive" extent of voter fraud that resulted in Trump's popular vote loss, or made-up terrorist attacks in Sweden. These, of course, are only a small sample of his ever-expanding corpus of lies. In a recent Sunday edition, the *New York Times*, much to its credit, tabulated all of Trump's lies in a full-page chart. In the give and take of breaking news and competition for scoops, however, pundits often fail to comment sufficiently on the overt and covert racism, bigotry, and xenophobia of our public figures.

When news attention shifts to foreign affairs, the ignorance of media figures is sometimes glaring. Most of our commentators know little to nothing about the complexities of Islam or the social and political schisms in the Islamic world. They show equal ignorance about the social and political dynamics of major players on the world stage: Russia, China, India, Pakistan, and Brazil, let alone other "lesser" societies in Europe, Latin America, Africa, and Asia. Such ignorance leads to ethnocentric judgments, which in turn produce misperceptions about the state of play in international politics. In our fast culture of expediency, who has the time to study the political dynamics of exotic societies or the philosophical foundations of a religion like Islam? In troubled times, expediency leads to dangerously shallow representation.

Writing an informed critique of an information-challenged media pundit can be tricky. If the critique is too esoteric or too detailed, it will have limited impact. If breaking news happens in a place where you have expertise and you find the coverage superficial or blighted with errors, then you should write a no-nonsense blog to set the record straight.

In the world of fast news, however, the record-straightening is often drowned out by pundits who continue to articulate their sometimes-well-intentioned misperceptions. Despite an ongoing critique, mainstream pundits often think Africa is one country rather than a vast continent constituting a complex array of heterogeneous ethnic groups that speak well over 2,000 linguistically distinct languages. In mainstream media representations, the "country" of Africa is a place where people lead miserable disease-ridden lives in war-torn spaces of incessant famine. As scholars, it is our obligation to set the record straight again and again. We should not do so, however, in posts that are filled with sneering sarcasm. A straightforward blog that demonstrates expertise contributes to a more powerful critique.

Since I've conducted the bulk of my ethnographic fieldwork in Africa, the blogs that follow are about how the media represents that continent. In these posts, I attempt to use plain language (clear sentences, fashioned into short paragraphs) to demonstrate how direct and long-term experience of (African) social life empowers a writer to present a more accurate representation of a society. In the blogs that follow, I attempt to demonstrate what an anthropological take on media punditry might mean for our comprehension of global social and political relations.

CHAPTER THIRTY TWO

MEDIA MATTERS IN AFRICA

(JANUARY 2012)

In a recent blog post, "Out of Africa," Patrick Smith, author of *Salon's* popular "Ask the Pilot" series, presented impressions of his latest trip to West Africa. "I love the flight into Dakar," Smith wrote, "but in Senegal I see how the world is falling to pieces right in front of me."

Smith went on to present his take on contemporary life in Senegal and other African nations, where, according to the blog, you must put up with bad service, exotically distasteful food, and sullen beggars who endlessly hit you up for gifts—food, clothing, or, better yet, money. Patrick Smith seems to have become disillusioned with Senegal. He wrote:

> Yet it's also true that the more time I've spent in Senegal, the less I've come to like it. The country has a way of beating you down, sucking your faith away. The heat, the garbage, the pickpockets and hustlers.
>
> Everybody hitting you up for something. Nobody smiling.

In the same piece, Smith described leaving a Lebanese restaurant and giving leftovers to a six- or seven-year-old child who was begging with a tomato can. He called the child a *talibe*, which he said refers to vagrant boys. In the blog post, he also described other places in West

Africa, writing about the garbage-strewn streets of Mopti in Mali where "naked children splash in greasy water," and a "surreal" drive to Kano, Nigeria.

> The topography is vaguely prehistoric—everything rendered a deep, almost putrefied green, with insanely jutting karsts reminiscent of Vietnam or the south of Thailand. The trees are clumped and gnarled. Goats, no dinosaurs.
>
> The man sitting next to the driver has an AK-47 and a Kevlar vest. He turns around and smiles.
>
> We tip him well.

What does Patrick Smith know of West Africa?

His commentary suggests a dangerously profound ignorance of things African. It's clear that Smith has spent only a few moments of time on the continent, hopping from airport to airport and occasionally taking tours to places like Mopti and Timbuktu. He doesn't know, for example, that *talibe* refers to a Quranic school student. These young boys are not vagrants, as Smith suggests, but live with Islamic clerics who teach them the Quran. In the evening, they beg for food. In Islam, it is a mark of piety to give food or money to the old, the infirm, the blind, and the maimed as well as to young Quranic school students.

The filth that Patrick Smith describes in Senegal and Mali is a result of poverty, which, of course, is not unique to West Africa. You can find hunger, filth, beggars, and shabby conditions in urban and rural America. In Nigeria, he describes a "prehistoric" landscape so much on the edge of criminal chaos that his taxi driver is escorted by a man wearing a Kevlar vest and carrying an AK-47.

This set of images paints an all too familiar portrait of social life in Africa. Smith's language suggests a backward, filthy, ramshackle, lawless, and humorless place that is beyond repair, a place where "the world is falling to pieces." This portrait, however, is only a minuscule part of the picture of social life in contemporary Africa. It describes surfaces not depths.

If Smith had spent more time in Senegal, Mali, or Niger, if he had attempted to speak to Africans in one of their own languages, if he had lived, even for a little while, with a Senegalese, Malian, or Nigerien family, his impressions might have been different.

Patrick Smith and I agree about one thing: you cannot deny the serious social and political problems in West Africa. Even so, if you get to know West Africans, you quickly realize that these problems don't sap their considerable social resilience. In my long study of things African, I've found that, despite the ravages of extreme poverty, most African people are somehow able to get on with their lives and make positive and sustainable contributions to their families, villages, and nations. The West Africans I've befriended over a 30-year period of research have come from all walks of life—urban professors, rural farmers, international traders, artisans, and university, high school and Quranic school students. I can't say I've liked all the people I've met in West Africa, but I can say that most of them have impressed me with their humor and their capacity to adapt and adjust to difficult conditions. What's most impressive, however, is their deep sense of social connection to one another.

This more humane dimension of African social life, however, is rarely discussed in the press. Patrick Smith's commentary of superficial impressions is, I'm afraid, much more common. Such a commentary creates a set of misleading perceptions about an entire continent, which, in turn, can lead to ethnocentric, if not racist, attitudes about people in Africa.

Patrick Smith's blogs appear to be popular. People like reading about a pilot's reflections on the adventure of air travel. But when it comes to representing the social lives of people, writers should take great care, for the power to represent is a great power, indeed, for it shapes our attitudes and beliefs, sometimes at great cost to those we are attempting to describe.

CHAPTER THIRTY THREE

JOSEPH KONY AND THE OTHER AFRICA

(MARCH 2012)

The continent of Africa is once again in the news. This time the buzz is about a viral video, *Kony 2012*, which is about the unspeakable atrocities committed by one Joseph Kony, leader of the Lord's Resistance Army in Uganda, which has consisted of a ragtag group of dazed and confused children who have been kidnapped. The girls become sex slaves and the boys are transformed into the child soldiers who mutilate their victims and sometimes are forced to kill their parents. In a matter of days, the video scored 50 million hits on the Internet. Although this is good news for Invisible Children, the organization that sponsored and showcased the video, it is more of the same when it comes to our narratives about the societies and cultures of Africa.

There can be no denial of the horrors of the Lord's Resistance Army or of Joseph Kony's horrendous crimes against humanity. By the same token, this film about the unimaginable violence that underscores social life in some parts of Uganda extends the notion that Africa, seen by most Americans and Europeans as one homogeneous country, is irreconcilably backward, brutish, and uncivilized. In this narrative, the country "Africa" is a place of failed government, incessant civil war, widespread famine, and boundless filth. It is a place where "Africans," irrational creatures, all have no history, no culture, and no religion—only the "law of the jungle." These Africans, who are destitute and barely human, need our help—to stop Joseph Kony or some other ruthless commander of an army of kidnapped children. While such activism may well result in the apprehension of a rebel leader, it also reinforces our stereotypical image of "Africa" and "Africans."

One of my obligations as an anthropologist who has spent more than 30 years learning from people who live in various parts of the African continent is to attempt to undermine destructive stereotypes. I never tire of informing people that Africa is not a country. Indeed, there are 54 sovereign nations in Africa. What's more, "Africans" don't speak "African." Indeed, people in Africa speak more than an estimated 2,000 languages—not dialects—that are grammatically distinct. As such, the continent of Africa is marked not by its homogeneity but by an almost mind-boggling diversity.

Such diversity is evident when you travel on the road that connects Niamey in Niger and Ouagadougou in Burkina Faso in West Africa. When you begin your journey, you are in Islamic Niger and the road cuts through an arid steppe dotted with acacia trees. Each town features a prominent mosque. This region is populated with Fulani and Songhay people, who tend to be tall and slender. After the border crossing you descend an escarpment and, after 10 kilometers, everything changes. There are vast plains of tall grasses and clusters of cottonwoods. The people who live on the plain, the Gurmantche, tend to be short and more round-bodied. In their towns, the most prominent structure is a church. Fulani, Songhay, and Gurmantche, of course, are mutually unintelligible languages. Accordingly, social and cultural life among these geographic neighbors is quite distinct. What's more, this diversity exists in a rather circumscribed geographic area.

So, Africa is not a country and Africans don't speak "African."

What about the most pernicious stereotype—that in the face of ongoing civil war and unending famine, "Africans" are powerless and need our help? The peoples of Africa are no strangers to drought and famine. Long before Europeans first traveled there, societies devised all sorts of ingenious social measures to deal with food shortages due to drought and/or famine. Clearly, funds to feed homeless and stateless families are much appreciated. But if you have lived among African peoples and speak one of the more than 2,000 African languages, what truly impresses—at least for me—is a capacity for social resilience—to confront adversity and adjust to it with verve and creativity.

This narrative is almost never recounted in the media or on the Internet. It is certainly not part of the *Kony 2012* narrative. How much does *Kony 2012* filmmaker Jason Russell know about social life in Uganda? Does he speak Baganda or one of the other languages spoken in that East African country? Has he lived there, or is his knowledge of the social life of Ugandan peoples simply a result of his visits and some background reading?

When you immerse yourself in the social life of another society and learn its language, you eventually learn how to ask central rather than peripheral questions. You are sensitized to what is important. You avoid falling into the trap of exoticism. Consider the following passage from Michael D. Jackson's compelling 2004 book, *In Sierra Leone*, a moving account that focuses on the impact of civil war on the social lives of people in that war-ravaged country. Like Uganda, Sierra Leone experienced the social and moral devastation of an army of kidnapped child soldiers who mutilated their victims. Sometimes these victims were forced to witness the brutal killing of their loved ones. Toward the end of the book, Jackson, an anthropologist who has spent more than 30 years thinking about Sierra Leonean social life, visits the Cline Town displaced persons camp, in which the orphans of war were trying to get beyond the horrors of their recent past. Conditions there were grim. And yet, despite their suffering, the young people there resiliently looked forward to new lives.

> What overwhelmed me was not the demands, nor the sense of impotence I felt, but the realization that these people needed so little to resume their lives, and that, rather than dwell on what had happened in the past, they desired only to move on, to start over. (Jackson 2004: 178)

Like the Sierra Leoneans that Jackson describes, the people I have known in Niger, Mali, Burkina Faso, and Senegal—not to forget those who live in the African diaspora—have impressed me deeply with their social and personal resilience. This resilience should be a much more important part of our narrative about the African continent.

The Sierra Leonean orphans of war—not Joseph Kony—merit 50 million hits on the Internet. Their stories mark a path toward a better life in the future.

CHAPTER THIRTY FOUR

MEDIA MYOPIA AND THE IMAGE OF AFRICA

(AUGUST 2013)

There seems to be no limit to the media's unwitting capacity to mis-characterize the African continent. Given the often inaccurate and superficial stories that emerge from Africa, is it any wonder that many people in the US, for example, think that Africa is one country? Is it any wonder that many Americans believe that the African continent is routinely ruled by greedy despots who live in extravagant luxury while their people suffer in the grip of poverty?

As I mentioned in several previous blogs on this sad subject, the print and broadcast media have usually constructed an African nar-rative of endless ethnic warfare, incessant drought, tragic famine, unspeakable epidemics, rampant rape, and chilling child abuse. The narrative also underscores dysfunctional family relations in which elderly patriarchs brutalize young women, some of whom may be their wives, some of who may be their daughters or nieces. In short, the media narrative about Africa makes it seem like a brutal place where people lead miserable lives, a place that is so destitute and hopeless that "we" need to "help" them.

These kinds of narratives embody partial truths about social life in Africa. There is no shortage of despots, epidemics, food insecurity, or family dysfunction in Africa. But for anyone who has spent time living with families in Senegal, Mali, Niger, Kenya, or Uganda, the narratives about social life in Africa become singularly complex—as complex as social life in American society. Indeed, the people I've met during more than 30 years of anthropological research in West Africa have been poor, but amazingly creative, resilient, and wise.

How, then, do these oversimplifications about Africa and Africans get established and reinforced?

Here's one example from Nicholas Kristof, internationally renowned columnist for the *New York Times*. In his July 13 column, "Where Young Women Find Healing and Hope," Mr. Kristof, whose important humanitarian work I greatly admire, described his visit to a medical center in Danja, Niger. Here's how Mr. Kristof began his "On the Ground" column about the fistula center:

> They straggle in by foot, donkey cart or bus: humiliated women and girls with their heads downcast, feeling ashamed and cursed, trailing stink and urine.
>
> Some were married off at 12 or 13 years old and became pregnant before their malnourished bodies were ready. All suffered a devastating childbirth injury called an obstetric fistula that has left them incontinent, leaking urine and sometimes feces through their vaginas. Most have been sent away by their husbands, and many have endured years of mockery and ostracism as well as painful sores on their legs from the steady trickle of urine.

It is incontestably important to bring into public awareness the problem of fistulas in Niger. But how much can Mr. Kristof—or anyone else—understand about the social and economic conditions of rural Niger if they simply "drop in" for a short visit to the Danja Fistula Center?

For many months, Alison Heller, a medical anthropologist, has been doing research at Niger's four fistula centers. She has studied Hausa, one of the two major languages in Niger, and knows the social and cultural history of the people who visit the Danja Fistula Center. In a recent entry to her blog, *Sai Hankuri: Fieldnotes from Niger*, she not only pinpoints the inaccuracies in Kristof's column but also suggests how they lead to stereotypical beliefs about Africa and Africans.

Responding to Kristof's lead sentence, "They straggle in by foot, donkey cart or bus: humiliated women and girls with their heads downcast, feeling ashamed and cursed, trailing stink and urine," Heller wrote:

> Women with fistula are incontinent, and although the severity of their leaks dramatically vary, they all leak. That said, most women with fistula meticulously tend to their self-care—adapting to their condition, creating homemade barriers or sanitary pads, washing diligently, slathering themselves in perfume. Very seldom can you smell a woman with fistula. Indeed, although they shoulder a heavy burden, they "trail" neither stink nor urine. In fact, many women go years without anyone knowing about their condition, including those closest to them, those with whom they share a house, or even a bed.

In the same July 13th column, Kristof wrote: "There is nothing more wrenching than to see a teenage girl shamed by a fistula," to which Heller responded:

> Nearly all of these "girls" have been married; nearly all have carried one or more pregnancies to term. Many sufferers of fistula are in their mid to late 20s, many in their 30s, and some in their 40s, 50s, 60s, and 70s. Does the suffering of a middle-aged woman with fistula count for less than the suffering of a "teenage girl"? Is it less "wrenching"?

In the column, Kristof tells the story of one of Danja's fistula patients, Hadiza Soulaye. Heller, who has talked with this woman over a long period of time, suggests that Kristof didn't recount her story correctly. She stated:

> Interviewing women about sensitive subjects can be diffi-cult. It takes time to grow a relationship and foster trust. On the surface, many women's stories seem the same—shame, pain, and hope for cure. But after picking and prodding

and posing and prying (a process that takes not just hours, but weeks and sometimes months), their stories take shape, holes are filled in, and the diversity of experiences begins to show itself. Still, it is too easy to cobble together a patchwork of facts with the thread of supposition. Reality fades into to fiction.

Heller's "on the ground" critique suggests a problem of much greater significance. Can we rely completely on generalist knowledge in an increasingly complex world? Can we send journalists—even ones as good as Nicholas Kristof—to faraway places where people speak unfamiliar languages like Songhay, Hausa, Tamasheq, and Wolof and expect them to quickly and fully understand what they are witnessing? This kind of quick representation often leads to negative stereotypes, mythical thinking, and misplaced priorities.

I am certainly not suggesting that Nicholas Kristof forgo travel to places like Niger. I applaud his efforts to raise life-changing funds for the Danja Fistula Center. To set the record straight, however, more scholars like Alison Heller need to bring their nuanced ground-level comprehension of complex social issues into the public sphere—one way to correct an epidemic of media myopia that creates and reinforces a fictive image of Africa.

CHAPTER THIRTY FIVE

MESSAGE FROM MALI

(MARCH 2015)

"There is no life without music," says Khaira Arby in the recent documentary, *They Will Have to Kill Us First*. Seeking refuge from Al-Qaeda-affiliated Islamists who in 2012 sacked Timbuktu's libraries, razed its shrines, and banned its music, Arby, the diva of the fabled city, fled to Bamako, Mali's capital, which is hundreds of kilometers from her home.

Safely ensconced in Bamako, Khaira Arby began to sing to assert her challenged cultural identity. Her story is not the exception among Mali's musicians from the north. In the wake of the Islamist assault, a new musically contoured cultural spirit has emerged. Although the Islamists in Northern Mali condemned moderate Sufism, destroyed UN cultural heritage sites in Timbuktu, and banned the magnificently rhythmic sounds of Takamba music (Desert Blues), the musicians, who are guardians of a great cultural tradition, assert that the music, a link to the ancestors, will not die.

The story of the new music group, Songhoy Blues, is a case in point. Andy Morgan, a journalist, wrote an article about Songhoy Blues in a December 2013 edition of the *Guardian*. He quotes Garba Touré, a guitarist with Songhoy Blues.

"The first rebel group to arrive were the MNLA [Mouvement National pour la Libération de l'Azawad], but they weren't against music, so there was no bad feeling between them and the population," he tells me over the phone from Bamako, Mali's capital. "But then Ansar Dine [a local armed Islamist group, whose name translates as "followers of the faith"] came and chased them out. They ordered people to stop smoking cigarettes, drinking alcohol and playing music. Even though I don't smoke or drink, I love the guitar, so I thought: 'This isn't the moment to hang around. I have to go south.'"

Like thousands of refugees, Garba grabbed a bag, his guitar and boarded a bus to Bamako. His father, Oumar Touré, a musician who had played congas for Mali's guitar legend, Ali Farka Touré, stayed behind with the family. The hardline Islamist gunmen drove music underground. The penalties for playing or even just listening to it on your mobile phone were a public whipping, a stint in an overcrowded jail or worse.

"When I arrived in Bamako the mood wasn't great," Garba remembers. "Different army factions were fighting each other. There were guns everywhere. All we heard was the scream of weapons. We weren't used to that."

Garba and some other musician friends from the north decided they couldn't succumb to the feeling that their lives had been shipwrecked by the crisis. They had to form a band, if for no other reason than to boost the morale of other refugees in the same situation. "We wanted to recreate that lost ambience of the north and make all the refugees relive those northern songs."

That's how Songhoy Blues was born....

The critics greeted the first album of Songhoy Blues, *Music in Exile* (February 2015), with rave reviews—a music inspired by forced dislocation. The music, which reminds me of the Takamba rhythms I heard 40 years ago in dusty compounds near the Niger-Mali border, is mesmerizing. The lyrics of the Songhoy Blues tunes reflect the wisdom of the Songhay people, especially when the musicians sing of patience (*soubour*) and courage (*faba*). In difficult times, Songhay elders often say that "life is patience," which is a profound take on the processes of history. Times may be bad right now, but if you walk your path with patience and courage, you will arrive in a better place. These songs, then, are a tonic that nourishes cultural resilience in northern Mali.

In February 2015, Songhoy Blues, Khaira Arby, Vieux Farka Touré, and Nick Zinner took this music in exile on the road. They traveled throughout the Sahelian region of West Africa with their Caravan of Peace. The aforementioned feature-length film *They Will Have to Kill Us First* documents this exercise in social and cultural resilience.

The music will not die.

These Malian musicians come from villages and towns that are war-ravaged, culturally challenged, and economically oppressed. These are places in which the average yearly income hovers around $300 a year. Even so the African peoples in the Sahel are not the hapless victims that our media describe in superficial African reports on famine, atrocities, and disease. Like most of the African people I've come to know during almost 40 years of contact, my Sahelian friends may be poor, but they are incredibly resilient.

When men and women dance to Takamba music they don the *boubou*, a billowing robe that Sahelian peoples wear with pride. Dressed in *boubous*, the music compels the dancers to sway their extended arms as if they were about to fly. In this way, they learn to take off, as they say in the Sahel, on the wings of the wind. "Flying" on the wings of the wind, they reconnect to the powers of patience, courage, and resilience.

We have much to learn from the Caravan of Peace and the likes of Khaira Arby and Songhoy Blues. As in Mali, there is no shortage of political and economic oppression in the United States. Considering the ever-growing celebration and extension of ignorance, intolerance, hate, and social violence, the prospect for our future generates no small measure of fear.

In our quest for a more perfect union will we learn the wise lessons of patience, courage, and resilience?

Will we learn how to fly on the wings of the wind?

PART FIVE

BLOGGING WELL-BEING: FINDING YOUR WAY IN TROUBLED TIMES

INTRODUCTION

There is no shortage of writers who publish books and print articles on health and well-being. These are often fashioned into illness narratives. How can a person confront physical adversity and squeeze from it a measure of well-being? Medical professionals, psychologists, and social workers write most of these widely read texts from a decidedly Euro-American orientation. The subject of health and well-being is also well represented on social media. Writers with personal blogs or those of us who publish pieces in *Psychology Today*, *Slate*, *Salon*, or *HuffPost* sometimes post about stress, aging, or vitamin regimens. Sometimes we craft illness narratives to communicate more generally about health and well-being.

As an anthropologist and scholar, I feel an obligation to discuss the nature of well-being in the world from a cross-cultural perspective. Since I am also a person who has been diagnosed with and treated for cancer, I am also compelled to write about how wisdom of the culture of one African society shaped my confrontation with cancer. Experiencing serious illness, in turn, prompted me to think long and hard about the quandaries of the human condition. Although I've written several books about my experience with cancer, those texts, if sales figures are indicative, did not reach large audiences. Hoping to convey my insights about illness to a larger audience, I began to publish *HuffPost* blogs about living with cancer. In these publicly posted personal blogs, I write about the ravages of illness but also about the quest for well-being.

Any published essay or book about personal experience—especially experience of illness—puts a writer on a slippery slope. A public blog about a personal confrontation with cancer, for example, carries many risks. Such a blog has the potential to reach a large audience. When that post goes "live," thousands of readers may learn about the intimacies of your life—your pain, your fears, your existential weaknesses. How specific should you be? What details should you leave out of an 850-word blog?

Here is the key issue in any personal narrative: will the reader connect the story to larger social, cultural, or political issues? Could that connection enhance well-being in the world? Narrowly defined personal blogs on public platforms are not likely to appeal to a broad audience of readers. Why should a reader who is not a friend or family member care about blood counts or side effects? If a personal blog about illness is short, brisk, evocative, and linked to larger social issues (the power of ritual in medical contexts (see Chapter 37) or the relation of illness to well-being (see chapters 39 and 40), it may attract wide reader interest and generate a flurry of both online and person-to-person conversation. This kind of blogging is yet another dimension of public anthropology in which the personal and professional are inextricably linked.

The posts that follow in this part of *Adventures in Blogging* demonstrate how anthropologists can introduce cross-cultural wisdom into the Eurocentric discourse about health and well-being. If this kind of blog is fashioned as a simply expressed narrative and posted on a public social media platform, it can bring a measure of comfort to people who are confronting the physical, emotional, and social discomforts of serious illness.

CHAPTER THIRTY SIX

LIVING WITH CANCER

(FEBRUARY 2011)

It was 10 years ago today that I was diagnosed with lymphoma, a cancer of the white blood cells. After more than a month of what seemed like an incessant number of suggestive but inconclusive diagnostic tests—blood work, sonograms, CT scans, and a CT-scan-guided biopsy—I was told that the grapefruit-sized tumor in my abdomen was filled with follicular lymphoma cells. I was informed that although follicular lymphoma—the most common subtype of non-Hodgkin lymphoma—responds well to treatment, it remains incurable.

In one day, my world was turned upside down. Until my diagnosis, I thought little about illness, and less still about my mortality. For years, I had followed a healthful regimen. I ate lots of fresh vegetables, consumed only small amounts of red meat, drank moderate amounts of alcohol, exercised regularly, and enjoyed a satisfying personal and professional life. I was not a prime candidate for cancer. And yet there I was, in a cold and sterile examination room—a relatively young man with an incurable disease. My life would never be the same.

Soon thereafter, I embarked on a path of aggressive treatment, very much relieved that the psychologically debilitating uncertainties of diagnosis were over. Like most people, I did not know what to expect from treatment. Chemotherapy was no cakewalk, but it did force me to change my routines. The world slowed down. What's more, in the treatment room I met an array of people whose quiet, unassuming "profiles in courage" both humbled and inspired me.

After nine months of treatment, CT scans indicated that I was in remission—a strange place to be. In remission, you are—for the most part—free of symptoms, but you are not "cured." Somewhere between sickness and health, you are told to come back every six months for CT scans to determine if you have remained cancer-free—or not. If you remain cancer-free, you make your way further into the nether world of remission. If the cancer has returned, as is often the case with follicular lymphoma, you begin a new regimen of treatments that continues until you get back into remission. If the treatments fail, you may try other treatment options, enter a clinical trial, or stop treatment altogether. In remission, you get to be like a defendant in court, waiting for what seems like a life or death verdict—not an easy place to be.

There is, of course, no perfect way for cancer patients to deal with such existential upheaval. Some people in remission become more religious. Others may change their occupations, learn a new language, take up a new hobby, or decide to travel more frequently. Because I'm an anthropologist, I attempted to cope with remission's uncertainties by revisiting my experiences as a young researcher in West Africa, where I spent many years as an apprentice to a traditional healer. That process eventually resulted in a book about my confrontation with cancer, *Stranger in the Village of the Sick: A Memoir of Cancer, Sorcery, and Healing*, in which I wrote about how West African ideas about illness and health helped me to confront cancer and cope with living in the sometimes confusing and always nebulous state between sickness and health—between what I like to call the village of the healthy and the village of the sick.

Ten years after the initial diagnosis, what can I say about living with cancer? When people sometimes suggest that I've "beat" cancer, or that I've put it put it behind me, I never agree. Once you've had cancer, I say to them, its presence never strays far from your awareness. Several years ago, during a public lecture I gave, someone in the audience asked, "Do you often think about cancer?" My answer was simple: "Every day."

If that sounds depressing, it's not. The specter of cancer has both negative and positive aspects. It can make you crabby and angry—the "why me?" syndrome. But because the presence of cancer makes you conscious of your mortality—something that most of us in mainstream American culture don't like to think about—it compels you to search and, in many cases, find what is truly important in life: contacting a lost friend, reinforcing family ties, traveling to a place you always dreamed of visiting, making some kind of contribution to the world. Looking back on the last 10 years, I can say that cancer prompted me to think much more about the future. It compelled me to try to meet the greatest obligation of West African healers: to pass knowledge on to the next generation, so that their lives might become just a little bit sweeter.

CHAPTER THIRTY SEVEN

REMISSION RITES

(FEBRUARY 2014)

More than 12 years ago, my oncologist gave me the great news that the non-Hodgkin lymphoma (NHL) that had been afflicting my body was in remission. After a grueling nine-month program of chemotherapy and immunotherapy, there was, he told me, no discernible trace of NHL in my body. The news made me leap for joy. I returned home to celebrate with loved ones. Champagne had never tasted so good!

Soon thereafter I came to the sober realization that remission is a slippery slope for cancer patients. Indeed, many friends, colleagues, and loved ones think that the state of remission means that you're cured, which, of course, is not the case for most cancers. Remission puts you in the indeterminate space between health and illness, a space that can be fraught with doubt, anxiety, and fear—of cancer's return.

Remission is a state in which your disease is "managed." During this period of physical and emotional limbo, you go for checkups at arranged intervals. From my anthropological vantage, I see these as remission rites. In my case the rites included blood work, a physical examination, and a CT scan, procedures that produced medical evidence that would be evaluated and discussed during a doctor visit. If the results of these rites were good I'd still be in remission, which meant that I would go through the same—or slightly modified—set of remission rites six months or one year later. If the results were not good, I'd reenter the prison house of treatment, hoping again, like Sisyphus, for a weary return to the state of remission.

Remission is sobering and taxing. But as you move along, the time between remission rites can become more or less normal. Everyday life can take on a pleasant routine. Your friends and loved ones no longer have to think so much about your disease. Some people you know may think that you have beat cancer or that you're a fearless survivor. Cancer patients can also fall into the false consciousness of having toughed it out, of having survived a painful ordeal, of having fought the enemy and won.

I certainly include myself in that all-too-common category. Ongoing remission gave me an unwavering confidence. At 10 years, I felt deep gratitude for an unexpected extension of my life. At 11 years, I knew that the uncertainties of remission would not slow me down. I still felt the passion to teach, the itch to travel, the desire to write more books, the wherewithal to initiate a research project, and the perseverance to produce a documentary film.

Even so the specter of yet another remission rite always gave me pause. The remission rite is not unlike a trial, the verdict of which can unalterably change your life. Even though I had become a 12-year remission rite veteran, the prospect of going to the Cancer Center three months ago frightened me.

My doctor and I chatted about our travels and our families and friends. He asked me routine questions about night sweats and unusual lumps, none of which I had experienced. Then he palpated my body looking for swollen lymph nodes or other potential abnormalities—never a pleasant experience, especially if your physician finds something unexpected and says:

"What a minute, what's this?"

"What do you mean?"

"Let me feel that again." He examined my underarms and my elbow a second time. "You've got some swollen nodes. They're tiny, but they're there."

How ironic that this exchange was almost identical to the dialogue I shared 13 years earlier when my primary care physician discovered an abdominal tumor. It's funny how your life can be turned upside down in matter of seconds. The swollen nodes might have resulted from an infection or from the scratches I routinely get from roughhousing with my dog. By the same token, the swollen nodes might be a signal of lymphoma's return.

My doctor suggested we wait to see if the nodes would persist. Trying my best to live with such unforeseen uncertainty, I returned one month later. Physical examination revealed the ongoing presence of the nodes. He ordered blood work and a CT scan, which due to scheduling issues and snow delays took place late in January. During the holiday season my life took on an unexpected and unwanted twist, reminding me once again of remission's innumerable difficulties. I tried to be festive and I succeeded to some extent, but I couldn't completely shake the dread of cancer's potential return.

Having avoided CT scans for many years, the one I endured in late January proved exceedingly stressful. What would the results reveal? Would I again be a regular guest in the treatment room? As it turned out the CT scan was normal, which was great news—more champagne. This time the celebration was intense but short-lived. Given my medical history, I know that remission rites will be a permanent feature of my future, which means that my existential limbo will persist.

Even so, you can learn to live—and live well—in remission. Beyond its stresses and strains, remission can be a space of great creativity and insight, an arena of what John Keats called "negative capability"—learning to live with psychological and physical uncertainties. Indeed, my continuous state of existential limbo has enabled me to better understand the human condition, which is a good thing for an anthropologist.

Being a remission rites adept, however, does not make me a "fighter," a "warrior," or a "survivor." Like most cancer patients, the realities of remission make me a person who simply tries to live fully within the limits of his circumstances.

CHAPTER THIRTY EIGHT

REMISS ABOUT REMISSION

(APRIL 2015)

Last week millions of television viewers watched the Ken Burns production of *Cancer: The Emperor of All Maladies.* It is a magnificent documentary film that is based largely upon Siddhartha Mukherjee's Pulitzer Prize-winning book. In the book and the six-hour documentary that emerged from it, we are exposed to the biography of cancer, a tale that encompasses thorough medical histories, poignant descriptions of the failure and successes of clinical research as well as interviews with prominent cancer researchers who give bright forecasts for future courses of treatment. For dramatic effect these segments are intercut with a set of cancer illness narratives featuring patients—and their families—who represent the social diversity of contemporary America: young and old, male and female, white, black and brown.

The unsentimental juxtaposition of the history of cancer to the human drama that its social presence creates is wonderfully impressive. Even so, what message does this impressive film send to those of us—more than 14.5 million in the US according the 2014 report of the American Cancer Society—who continue to live with cancer, who continue to exist in a state between health and illness, who live in what the sociologist Arthur Frank has called the "remission society"? Aside from the story of one long-term cancer patient who, despite being "cancer-free" for more than 20 years, doesn't feel completely "healed," there is little mention of what life is like for patients who are free of symptoms but not cured.

Like most of the 14.5 million Americans who are in some phase of cancer remission, I am profoundly grateful to the dedicated scientists and clinicians who have worked hard and well to improve current conditions for effective treatment and future prospects for cures. It is not difficult to understand the physical and psychological troubles of patients who are being diagnosed with or treated for cancer. Through no choice of their own, these individuals are compelled to face the prospect of their mortality—no easy matter for clinicians, patients, or family members. In the six-hour documentary, these elements are presented with powerful nuance and great skill. It is perhaps much more difficult to try to capture the murkiness of remission, a state in which patients are betwixt and between health and illness.

The much-hyped documentary, which is certain to win great praise and many rightfully deserved awards, represents mainstream immunological thinking about disease, a system of thought that is consistent with our narratives about health and illness. For most Americans, health is a steady state that illness—or dis-ease—periodically disrupts until our immune systems—sometimes on their own and sometimes with the aid of increasingly powerful targeted medicines—get us back to a normal situation in which we feel little or no discomfort, in which we are not pondering our mortality. In immunological thinking, illness is other—something that invades our bodies and triggers physical and emotional havoc in our lives. Illness is the enemy that we must obliterate so we might regain the steady state of health and well-being. In a sense the immunological treatment of illness is a battle, or in the case of cancer, a war that must be waged on many fronts.

In this system of thought, if you win the battle—which, in the scope of things, is usually the case—you eventually regain your health. If you lose a series of battles, however, you begin a descent into pain, disease, and a potentially premature death. Indeed, the last two-hour segment of *Cancer: The Emperor of All Maladies* is all about immunology—how researchers can use the genetic mapping of tumors to design cancer vaccines that trigger immune responses that can annihilate cancer cells. Such a regimen is a powerful way to treat cancers.

If improved treatment is making cancer a more "manageable" set of disorders, and if such "management" has made remission the everyday reality of 14.5 million Americans, why is so little attention devoted to remission in a documentary like *Cancer: The Emperor of All Maladies?* Why is there not a similarly hyped documentary on the trials and tribulations of post-treatment depression, of people failing to comprehend your cancer experience, of the unending cascade of friends and family who say "you beat it," when you know that "it" can return at any moment?

These questions force us to confront more fully the social and cultural dimensions of illness and health. From an anthropological vantage, many aspects of the remission experience are counter-cultural. They are more consistent with anthropologically documented non-Western orientations to disease in which illness is not the enemy, but a companion who can step into your life at any moment and unalterably change the circumstances of your existence. In these orientations you take active measures to treat your illness. And if you become a member of the "remission society," you engage in activities that make remission's uncertainties more bearable. In so doing, you accept the limitations that your condition presents and try to live fully within them, an action that can bring to even the most compromised member of the "remission society" a measure of well-being.

As *Cancer: The Emperor of All Maladies* attests, we have made great advancements in the diagnosis and treatment of cancer, advancements that have ironically produced cultural narratives that tend to limit our comprehension of the considerable social and cultural ramifications of *The Emperor of All Maladies.* Greater cross-cultural awareness of the relationship of illness to well-being may compel us to pay more attention to the important life-changing quandaries of remission in addition to the physical and emotional dimensions of cancer diagnosis and treatment.

CHAPTER THIRTY NINE

WELL-BEING IN THE WORLD

(FEBRUARY 2015)

On these dark and dreary February days the news has been hard to stomach. The brutality of videotaped ISIS executions has been gut-wrenching. In the Ukraine, there's no end in sight for a desolate war. In the US, the ongoing distrust of medicine (the vaccination controversies) and climate science (human-instigated climate change is a "hoax") is dispiriting, especially as we hear more and more dire predictions about our bleak environmental future. In the social arena, income inequality continues to increase.

It is increasingly clear that our social and political ignorance is pushing us closer and closer to despoiling our planet. Chances are that we will bequeath to our children and grandchildren a hellish world of droughts, floods, super storms, epidemics, and massive social dislocation.

What is this world coming to?

Despite the sweep of doom-and-gloom news, I sometimes wake up on cold and dark February mornings and think about well-being. The conventional approach to studies of well-being is one that seeks to measure factors that create the infrastructural context for a well-lived life. United Nations' Human Development Index researchers use a matrix of objective well-being measurements, like per-capita income and life expectancy, to rate the "livability" of nations. These ratings, however, appear to have limited applicability. In an Associated Press report of Dec. 19, 2012, Michael Weisserman wrote about an intriguing Gallup survey on happiness in the world.

> The world's happiest people aren't in Qatar, the richest country by most measures. They aren't in Japan, the nation with the highest life expectancy. Canada, with its chart-topping percentage of college graduates, doesn't make the top 10.
>
> A poll released Wednesday of nearly 150,000 people around the world says seven of the world's 10 countries with the most upbeat attitudes are in Latin America...
>
> Many of the seven do poorly in traditional measures of well-being, like Guatemala, a country torn by decades of civil war followed by waves of gang-driven criminality that give it one of the highest homicide rates in the world. Guatemala sits just above Iraq on the United Nations' Human Development Index, a composite of life expectancy, education, and per capita income. But it ranks seventh in positive emotions...
>
> Prosperous nations can be deeply unhappy ones. And poverty-stricken ones are often awash in positivity, or at least a close approximation of it.

This finding suggests what anthropologists have long known: Human well-being emerges less from objective economic or sociological indicators than from the quality of our social relations—the texture of social life.

I've learned most of what I know about well-being from people we'd least expect to experience it, the Songhay of the Republic of Niger, the poorest nation in the world. How can it be that people who usually earn less than one dollar a day and live in ramshackle mudbrick houses—most of which lack electricity, running water, and indoor plumbing—know something about well-being? How can people who must struggle every day to feed their frail children look forward to a new day during which they will greet their friends and manage to laugh with their neighbors? Considering the monumental challenges they face, many Songhay people, I have come to realize, have become masters of practical wisdom.

Here's some of what I've learned from my Songhay friends in Niger.

1. **Well-being is social**. If your central mission in life is to establish and maintain good social relations in your family, neighborhood, and community, you will experience the well-being of knowing that no matter the circumstance you are not alone in the world.

2. **Well-being is fleeting**. We are always seeking the pleasurable and complete feeling that is associated with well-being, but such moments are fleeting. Sweet moments of contentment should be savored and appreciated, but are over in a flash. Because those moments are so wonderful, our quest for them never ends.

3. **Well-being is limited**. No one can live a perfect life. If you accept some of the limitations that life has presented, as, for example, living in rural Niger, you can live well within those limits and extract from them profound moments of well-being.

These ideas are more than quaint expressions of an esoteric scholarly exercise. They can be applied to our personal and social lives. They can certainly be applied to the politics of the public sphere that is in dire need of periodic infusions of well-being.

The anthropological record is filled with this kind of important knowledge. A small slice of practical wisdom from an isolated and impoverished corner of the world is no panacea for our social, environmental, and political problems. Even so, this wisdom can bring to us those brief moments of sweetness that make life, no matter how challenged, worth living.

A PATH TOWARD WELL-BEING

(FEBRUARY 2016)

It's been 15 years since I learned that I had non-Hodgkin lymphoma, a set of blood cancers, which, as they say, can be managed but not cured. When I received this devastating news, I thought that my relatively short life would soon be over. How could someone like me, a trim, active man who had a healthy diet, a lovely family, a terrific set of friends and a satisfying professional life, get cancer?

It didn't make sense.

It made me angry.

The news stunned me. My bleak future flashed before my eyes— chemotherapy, weight loss, hair loss, bone pain, nausea, and fatigue— all leading to an untimely death. I suddenly realized how much time I had wasted on unimportant things. Confronting imminent mortality frightened me. Slowly and timidly, I moved forward on an uncertain path. In the time that I had left, could I somehow experience the wonders of life? In a world of endless choice and incessant distraction, could I discover what was important?

Given our culturally contoured and time-pressed penchant for expedience, it's hard for anyone to figure out what is important. A diagnosis of cancer, though, can sometimes accelerate a process that sometimes points you in an existentially satisfying direction. A 15-year sojourn on cancer's path has compelled me to think about how to live well in the world. Here are some of things I've learned about the quest for well-being:

1. **The destructive force of anger**. When I began my journey on cancer's path, I was angry. Why had I been singled out to suffer such a horrendous fate? I quickly discovered that anger led to feelings of powerlessness and despair, a state that wasn't good for me, for the people around me, or for my work as a scholar. In my view anger never leads to well-being. And so I tried to accept my situation and attempted to cope with the anxieties of confronting an incurable disease—none of which is easy.

2. **Combating bad faith**. In his incomparable play, *No Exit*, Jean-Paul Sartre confronts the specter of bad faith, a collective set of beliefs based on illusion. In bad faith, we construct the world as we want it to be, which blinds us to the world as it is. In bad faith, we make life choices based on wishful fantasy rather than inconvenient truth. The political world is rife with bad-faith thinking and decisions—the fateful decision to wage war in Iraq, the denial of climate change, the dogged belief in supply-side economics, and the distrust of science. In the world of cancer, bad-faith thinking and decision-making can compel people to deny their medical status. It can convince people to seek unproven miracle cures. The negative results of bad-faith thinking also tend to reinforce anger, which in turn leads to bitterness. Long before I understood much about anything, Adamu Jenitongo, a wise man among the Songhay people of West Africa, taught me to consider a situation realistically. He said that a person needs to accept her or his limitations and live well within the parameters those limitations set. That advice only made sense to me when I had to consider how remission from cancer, a way station between health and illness, between life and death, limited my possibilities in the world. Those limitations, I soon discovered, did not prevent me from living well in the world.

3. **The importance of human connection**. If you live in isolation, chances are you will construct a world shaped by bad faith. If you have the good-faith support of friends and family, you are likely to confront your remission realistically, a position that allows for a life filled with

little as well as big pleasures. It is well known that social isolation often leads to alcohol and drug abuse as well as to a variety of domestic dysfunctions. It is also well known that the absence of social support contributes to heath declines and premature mortality. No one should be alone when confronting the physical and emotional challenges of cancer diagnosis, treatment, and remission.

4. **The value of patience.** In America, we live in a time-pressed, impatient, results-oriented society. We take the furiously fast straight highway—not the slow sinuous side road—to get from one place to another. We expect such an emphasis in the corporate world, but we also find it in academe. In academe, there is an emphasis on results. Did you get the grant? Did you publish in one of the most prestigious journals? Are your ideas cutting-edge? How many books have you published in the last five years? Are you on the fast track to a distinguished career? When you begin treatment for cancer, no matter who you might be, the world slows down. You can continue to do elementary things like walk or get out of bed, but you have to do them slowly, deliberately, and mindfully. When you undergo chemotherapy, you have to sit in a chair for long periods of time—two, three, or, in my case, five hours. The side effects of treatment demand a slower orientation to life; they require patience. This slow approach to learning is consistent with apprenticeship in West Africa, during which novices spend 10, 20, or even 40 years slowly mastering their art or their science, patiently waiting for their paths to open. When they do, they are ready to make important contributions to the world.

I don't know what the future will bring. I do know that patience shows us the way to a path that opens to the world. On the open path, we understand how to proceed. With clarity of purpose we take small but confident steps. Along this path, we understand what we can do in the world. Comfortable in our skins, we savor a measure of well-being. That profound feeling leads us to expressions of deep gratitude, which are answered, in turn, with the embrace of human warmth.

For me, that is a path worth following.

EPILOGUE: ANTHROPOLOGY AND POPULAR MEDIA

So much has changed since I defended my Ph.D. dissertation more than three decades ago. When I wrote my thesis, most graduate students used IBM electric typewriters to compose their theses. What's more, the end product had to conform to a standard template. Indeed, one of the most feared people at the University of Texas at Austin, where I pursued graduate studies in social anthropology, was the guardian of that template, a woman who worked in the graduate school office. Having laboriously produced a putatively error-free, fully edited 330-page document, I presented it to her with great trepidation. She took hold of my dissertation, gave me a steely-eyed stare, and vowed to look at all the pages to see if they conformed to the strictly enforced representational criteria. If a sentence was one or two characters too long, she informed me, the page and/or pages would have to be retyped. If there were glaring misspellings or word omissions, they, too, would have to be corrected—sometimes with a mysterious fluid called Wite-Out. If Wite-Out proved to be too messy, as was often the case, then the page or pages, depending on the location of the error, would also have to be retyped. Given the privations of these representational conditions, it's a wonder that scholars and graduate students somehow managed to produce doctoral theses, journal articles, and books.

We now live in a digital age in which electronic connectedness is increasingly giving shape and texture to human relationships. (See Carr 2011; Gladwell 2008; Griffiths 1998; Castells 2009; Keen 2012; and Rettberg 2014.) Scholars have long assumed a direct relationship between technological innovation and social change. The invention of the printing press helped to propel the vulgarization of national languages (English, French, German), a development that eventually challenged Latin as the language of scholarship. The inventions of the telescope and microscope refined scientific method and deepened knowledge of the outer workings of the cosmos and the inner workings of the human body. These innovations contributed to the Copernican Revolution as well as the germ theory of disease. The introduction of the steam engine, telegraph, telephone, automobile, and airplane, of course, added new dimensions to our social relations and reshaped our social institutions—the family, the community, the state, the international order.

At the conclusion of his highly readable book, *The Digital Turn: How the Internet Transforms Our Existence* (2013), Wim Westera wrote:

> We have to accept that digital media irreversibly change our habitat. They create new extensions of reality, along with new representations, altered identities, and new forms of being. How should we deal with this? Negation is not an option since it requires us to exclude ourselves from the core of society's processes.
>
> Unconcerned adoption is likewise hazardous because of misconceptions, improper expectations, and unclear risks. We may easily lose ourselves in the illusions of the virtual realm.
>
> The only option is to become media literate. We should involve our unique cognitive abilities to remain in control of it, just as we successfully defeated our predators and survived disasters and other adversities. We should all possess true and deep understanding of the risks associated with the media that confront us. (p. 251)

Westera goes on to suggest:

> Essentially, media literacy is not so much about media. It is about the ways we interact with media and derive meaning

from it. The ultimate consequences of the mirror metaphor of media is that the complexity of media reflects of the complexity of our selves. By understanding media, we will get to know ourselves. (p. 253)

As we adjust ourselves to digital complexities, how can scholars adapt to a new set of representational realities? In *Adventures in Blogging* I've attempted to show—rather than tell—that blogging is central to the future of social science. Even so, it is not the only medium of future scholarly expression. In the 21st century, public anthropologists, for example, will have a wide choice of media to communicate culture. In addition to blogging, these include narrative ethnography, fiction, ethnographic film/video, performance, poetry, and multimedia art installations.

NARRATIVE ETHNOGRAPHY

Although many anthropologists continue to communicate culture through the theoretically foregrounded academic monograph, the anthropological gift to the world continues to be ethnography, the detailed description of a social order. In truth, many of these are anthropological texts that attract a limited readership. When an ethnographic text works, however, it can be magical, for it can sensuously connect readers to a place and its people. In these relatively rare ethnographic works, the writer crafts a work in which the textured world of others explodes from pages that feature laboriously crafted dialogue as well as sensuously evoked place and character. These texts, which foreground narrative, are complex and nuanced works that attract readers as well as publishers eager to bring to life books with legs, books that will powerfully communicate culture well into the 21st century (see Narayan 1989; Behar 2007; Stoller 2014; Jackson 2004; and Allen 2011, among many others).

FICTION

Fiction and narrative ethnography share many features. In both fiction and narrative ethnography, writers strive to evoke place and space, creating a feel for a location. In both fiction and narrative ethnography, authors attempt to develop a sense of character. What is distinctive about a particular people? Is it the way they walk, a particular facial expression, the way they comport themselves? Is it the way they talk to others? These features contribute to a work's appeal that compels readers to turn the page.

There are, of course, differences between narrative ethnography and fiction. In contrast to ethnography, fiction writers and graphic novelists can configure image, dialogue, and narrative to build plot. They can also write inner dialogue, expressions of a character's silent thoughts and desires. Fiction writers and graphic novelists use these techniques to put the reader in a lock hold of attention that, if well done, is not released until the last page is reached. Fiction writers and graphic novelists who tap into ethnographic knowledge to recount a story are able to communicate culture to a wide audience of readers—a path toward a public anthropology. Scholars have long predicted the end of the novel. Considering the ongoing popularity of fiction and an ever-expanding audience for graphic novels, this genre is very much with us and is likely to be a force for cultural storytelling well into the future. (See Jackson 1986; Narayan 1994; Stoller 1999, 2005, 2016; and Hamdy and Nye 2017, among many others.)

ETHNOGRAPHIC FILM/VIDEO

The late, great Jean Rouch liked to extol the virtues of ethnographic film. During a trip from Niamey, Niger, to Accra, Ghana, he hung a copy of his book on the Songhay-Zarma migrations to Ghana—part of his doctoral dissertation—from the rear-view mirror of his car.

How many of the subjects of that study would read the book? he wondered.

Not many, he reasoned. But if those same subjects saw his classic work, *Les Maitres Fous* (1955), they would immediate understand the language of film. By way of film, Rouch would often argue, anthropological insights on colonialism, racism, migration, nationalism, and the construction of identity could reach a large and varied audience. Rouch paved the way for ethnographic filmmakers to depict social difference that makes a difference in the world of policy and politics. Film, then, has been a strong and important element in the practice of public anthropology. (See Rouch 1955; Stoller 1992.)

In the digital age, film/video has become an integral part of social media. Given the small size and reasonable costs of video cameras and the accessibility of high-quality editing software, it has never been easier and more cost-effective to make film/videos. What's more, contemporary filmmakers can easily upload their trailers and finished works onto Facebook, YouTube, and Vimeo, three platforms that enable the wide circulation of filmic material that represent anthropologically important subjects. These new forms of filmic distribution constitute yet another felicitous path toward a more public anthropology.

PERFORMANCE

Performance is an effective way to present ethnographic research to the public. It is exceeding difficult to write monologue/dialogue, let alone produce a work in which monologue/dialogue is the only vehicle for the development of plot and drama. When performance works, it is a powerful way to convey anthropological insights to the general public. One recent example of an anthropologically contoured play is *The Man Who Almost Killed Himself*, a play directed by Josh Azouz (2014). The play emerged from Andrew Irving's anthropological research on the social lives of HIV/AIDS patients in Uganda and New York City (see Irving 2017).

Illness and how we confront mortality are serious anthropological subjects. Such existential elements are ripe for transformation into widely appealing dramatic narratives. Such is the case with the play *The Man Who Almost Killed Himself*, the main character of which is a Ugandan man who tries to kill himself but never succeeds. Each time the protagonist attempts suicide he is undermined by a 5000-year-old God, who cheerfully finds ways for *The Man Who Almost Killed Himself* to remain among the living.

"*The Man Who Almost Killed Himself*," theater critic Andy Currums writes, "is a fascinating and funny journey through the cultural and political recent history of Uganda and Africa—a history that still sends ripples through to the modern day" (Currums 2014).

The play premiered at the Edinburgh Theatre Festival in August 2014 and was broadcast on BBC Arts and featured at Odeon Cinemas. The play demonstrates how ethnographically nuanced drama can bring anthropological insights on race, diversity, health and illness, and religion to large and diverse audiences.

POETRY

Many anthropologists have written inspirational poetry. Great anthropological pioneers like Ruth Benedict published poetry. The tradition continues into the present with exemplary works by Ruth Behar, Dennis Tedlock, Melisa Cahnmann-Taylor, Lila Abu-Lughod, Jerome Rothenberg, Valentine Daniel, Adrie Kusserow, Michael Jackson, Renato Rosaldo, Noni Stone, and Gina Ulysse. What is it about poetry that captures the imagination?

On several occasions, I've had the privilege of listening to Renato Rosaldo read his poems. Speaking softly and reading with quiet emotion, Rosaldo's dignified presence gave powerful substance to his words, which created an event in which the connection between the poet, Rosaldo, and the audience became palpable. Consider this short poem and how it speaks powerfully to the sensuous ethnographic realities of the Philippines, the place where he and his late wife, Michelle Zimbalist Rosaldo, conducted fieldwork.

No Swimmer
The river turns brown,
swells, churns, rises, slants.
No raft rides its surface
no swimmer dares its current.
On high ground men and women teeter
as if on a precipice.
Persistent rumors,
Soldiers at checkpoints torture suspects
bodies mutilated bullet-riddled. (Rosaldo 2014: 43)

Consider Rosaldo's commentary about the work of poetry:

> The work of poetry, as I practice it, is to bring its subject—
> whether pain, sorrow, shock, or joy—home to the readers.
> It is not an ornament; it does not make things pretty. Nor
> does it shy away from agony and distress. Instead it brings
> things closer, or into focus, or makes them palpable. It slows
> the action, the course of events, to reveal depth of feeling
> and to explore its character. It is a place to dwell and savor
> more than a space for quick assessment. (2014: 105)

Poetry, then, is a slow and heartfelt practice that palpably extends anthropological insights to the public.

MULTIMEDIA ART INSTALLATIONS

The advent of the ethnographically inspired multimedia art installation is an important new development in the human sciences. Multidisciplinary collaborative teams are creating works that fuse art and social science through multisensorial and multidisciplinary installations. Such work has contributed profoundly to a more public anthropology in which scholarly insights about the human condition are being communicated powerfully and intelligently to the general public. In a culture of speed and expedience, this kind of public representation is an important development in the social sciences and humanities. The Ethnographic Terminalia (ET) (2009–2014) is a case in point.

As previously stated, we stand today at a threshold. How will scholars adapt their practices to the expanding digital realities of the 21st century? That which was separate in the past (the arts and humanities, the social and natural sciences) can now be productively and imaginatively integrated. Artistic works can also be linked electronically to textual passages in social media platforms, creating spaces of sensory integration, design creativity, and evocative power. In the 21st century can we say that it is sufficient to limit social science practice to protocols of standard observation, data collection, and induction, all leading to objective and dispassionate theorization in academic texts? The academic monograph remains an important measure of scholarly evaluation. Even so, in a digitally integrated world, as I have attempted to show in *Adventures in Blogging*, other forms of representation (blogs, memoir, fiction, poetry, film/video, soundscapes, and multimedia installations) that fuse the power of the arts and social sciences are becoming increasingly important.

For seven years ET has playfully explored "reflexivity and positionality," asking "what lies beyond disciplinary territories. No longer content to subordinate the sensorium to theoretical and expository monographs, ET is a curatorial collective motivated by possibilities of new media, locations, and methods" (Ethnographic Terminalia Collective 2009). In all the ET installations, the curatorial collective suggests that "[t]he terminus is the end, the boundary, and the border. It is also a beginning, its own place, a site of experience and encounter. Ethnographic Terminalia exhibits new forms of anthropology engaged with contemporary art practice" (ibid.).

To present a glimpse of the power and importance of ET's work, consider the 2014 installation, *The Bureau of Memories: Archives and Ephemera*, which focused on an important anthropological and historical subject of study: the nature of memory. How do we remember the past? For many peoples in the world, history has a powerful tactile dimension. In my review of that exhibit, I wrote: "With its inclusively tactile and multisensorial dimensions, the exhibition demonstrates the central importance of a new wave of anthropological expression, an articulation that fuses past and present and here and there. In short, *The Bureau of Memories* invites us to glimpse into the future and provides a much-appreciated tonic for the public dimensions of our discipline" (Stoller 2015).

IS PUBLIC ANTHROPOLOGY PUBLIC ENOUGH?

At the beginning of *Adventures in Blogging* I stated that the discipline of anthropology has had a long history of public engagement. In his aforementioned campaign against the racism and Social Darwinism of early 20th-century America, Franz Boas demonstrated the power of public anthropology. The public dimension of anthropology has also been represented in museum exhibitions, which continue to introduce anthropology to the general public. It is not far-fetched to say museum exhibit halls are the spaces in which millions of people are exposed to anthropological knowledge.

As a discipline, anthropology has therefore had a deep and ongoing connection to "the public." Given the depth and breadth of public anthropological engagement, it would seem that anthropological ideas would have attracted a great deal of attention in the public sphere. The discipline did produce the likes of Margaret Mead, who in her books, magazine columns, and public lectures deftly communicated anthropological ideas to the general public. And yet it seems to me that too much anthropological wisdom remains hidden in in the impenetrable prose of journal articles and academic monographs.

Can we link a venerable scholarly tradition to a world in which swift and ever-changing digital technologies have shaped a culture of speed? In a 2014 *Chronicle of Higher Education* essay entitled "Speed Kills," philosopher Mark Taylor worries that digitalization has produced social and economic acceleration from which has emerged "fast culture." No one can deny the many positive features of speedy technology. But speed has many drawbacks. We seem to read less, as Taylor asserts, and have less time to think and reflect. Perhaps the most important drawbacks of fast culture, as noted in chapters 21 and 22 of *Adventures in Blogging*, are social alienation and cultural isolation. Consider Taylor's words:

> As I have noted, technologies that were designed to connect us and bring people closer together also create deep social, political, and economic divisions. The proliferation of media outlets has led to mass customization, which allows individuals and isolated groups of individuals to receive personalized news feeds that seal them in bubbles with little knowledge of, or concern about, other points of view.

Taylor's point raises the question: are our ideas and insights produced for only limited consumption? Even if an increasing number of scholars have mastered the art of long-form public blogging, who is reading what we write? Many of the websites devoted to contemporary anthropology (*Anthropology Now*, *Savage Minds* [now *Anthrodendum*], *SAPIENS*, *HAU*, *Living Anthropologically*, *Anthropologyworks*, *Allegra Lab*, and *Somatosphere*) are usually focused on traditional anthropological topics. In a recent issue of *SAPIENS*, perhaps the anthropology website with the largest Internet coverage, consider what the editors highlighted as the "most popular" contributions: "Confederates in the Amazon," "Paleolithic Ax Debunks Colonial Myth," "Uncovering Ancient Clues to Humanity's First Fires," "Why Do We Keep Using the Word 'Caucasian'?" and "Is the Term 'People of Color' Acceptable?" Websites like *SAPIENS* are spreading the anthropological word across the Internet. Indeed, they are an integral part of public anthropology. But is this digitally based public anthropology public enough?

The troubling realities of contemporary fast culture require a fresh approach to scholarly engagement. An increasing number of anthropologists, among other social scientists, want to contribute to public debate about the issues of our times: the persistence of racism, ethnic discrimination, Islamophobia, gender bias and homophobia, the everexpanding specter of income and social inequality, and the ongoing battle against ignorance that is linked to the denigration of science.

Here's the issue: most scholars, including, of course, most anthropologists, do not write clear and compelling prose. Perhaps the greatest key to developing a truly public anthropology lies less in adopting increasingly sophisticated digital platforms than in training scholars to write for broader audiences. With doses of constructive guidance, anyone can learn to write well—for the general public.

How do you write clear and crisp sentences?
How can you evoke space and place?
How do you write dialogue?
What techniques can you use to craft a personal portrait?

These, of course, are the central ingredients of narrative, which can be used in a variety of genres—including blogs—to communicate culture.

In the education of scholars, public writing courses have not been part of disciplinary curricula. Even so, a number of writing workshops are available to scholars who want to share their ideas with the general public. At many professional conferences, there are workshops on poetry, creative nonfiction, public writing, and public blogging. These are usually of short duration—two- to three-hour sessions—squeezed into fully programmed three-to-four-day gatherings. Frankly, two to three hours is not enough time to develop public writing skills. A number of writers have designed more comprehensive workshops. Tapping into my experience as a writer, I developed a three-day public writing workshop, "Weaving the World," which features exercises in transforming academic prose into plain language, evoking place, writing dialogue, and crafting character. We also have blogging sessions. These workshops, which I have run for more than four years, have worked quite well. At the end of three very intense days, most of the participants have been encouraged to write their stories more evocatively. In some cases, participants developed blogs that they posted on public websites. No matter the genre, if you make a sustained effort to write anthropology for public consumption, as I like to tell workshop participants, the practice will make you a better writer.

To help us confront the representational challenges of our times, more of these workshops should be developed. Better yet, our institutions, as Alisse Waterston has suggested, need to valorize public writing by (1) integrating this practice into our graduate curricula and (2) "getting credit" for doing public anthropology. In the end, public anthropology is not yet public enough, but has the potential to become a potent force in future debate. My hope is that *Adventures in Blogging* demonstrates how posting accessible, anthropologically contoured blogs on social media platforms can help to make the world more politically, socially, and culturally informed.

THE POWER OF THE STORY

Amid all the discussions about public anthropology and the impact of digital technologies on the future representation of social worlds, there is one central theme that should not be overlooked or underestimated: the profound importance of stories and storytelling. In the 1980s I had the rare privilege of attending film screenings in

Jean Rouch's makeshift projection room above his office in the Musée de l'Homme in Paris. Rouch would routinely gather an eclectic group of people to chime in on a film's strengths and weaknesses. During those sessions, Rouch would invariably ask about the narrative character of the film.

Is the story a good one? Does it work?
Will the story connect with the audience?
If the story doesn't work, can a better one be imagined?

For me, our capacity to imagine, create, anticipate, and speculate about the social world emerges from a central source: the story. Does the narrative inspire? Does it make us think new thoughts and feel new feelings? Does it connect with the public and compel people to imagine the future?

Rouch's questions are still important in an expanding world of representation. Can we find stories in sensuously contoured photographs, soundscapes, films, poetry, in multimedia installations or in blogs? Do those stories establish links between the artist-anthropologist and her or his audience?

These are exciting times—new electronic platforms, digital innovation, and evolving forms of scholarly and artistic representation. In the passion of the representational moment, however, it is easy to forget Jean Rouch's central question.

Where is the story?

No matter the representational format, no matter the platform, no matter the multisensorial sophistication of the representational design, if there is no story, what is there?

WORKS CITED

Allen, Catherine. 2011. *Foxboy: Intimacy and Aesthetics in Andean Stories*. Austin: University of Texas Press.

Anderson, Ryan, and Sarah Kendzior. 2013. "Interview: Sarah Kendzior." *Savage Minds* (blog), May 12, 2013. https://savageminds.org/2013/05/12/savage-minds-interview-sarah-kendzior/.

Azouz, Josh. 2014. *The Man Who Almost Killed Himself*. London: HiBrow Productions.

Behar, Ruth. 2007. *An Island Called Home: Returning to Jewish Cuba*. New Brunswick, NJ: Rutgers University Press.

Berg, Maggie, and Barbara K. Seeber. 2016. *The Slow Professor: Challenging the Culture of Speed in the Academy*. Toronto: University of Toronto Press.

Carr, Nicholas. 2011. *The Shallows: What the Internet Is Doing to Our Brains*. New York: W.W. Norton.

Castells, Manuel. 2009. 2nd ed. *The Rise of the Network Society*. New York: Wiley-Blackwell. https://doi.org/10.1002/9781444319514.

Currums, Andy. 2014. "Review of *The Man Who Almost Killed Himself*." Broadway Baby. http://broadwaybaby.com/shows/the-man-who-almost-killed-himself/702204.

Dunleavy, Patrick. 2013. "Paper books in a digital era: How conservative publishers and authors almost killed off books in university social science." *LSE Review of Books*, April 29, 2012.

Ethnographic Terminalia Collective. 2009–2014. *Ethnographic Terminalia*. Washington, DC: American Anthropological Association.

Gladwell, Malcolm. 2008. *Outliers: The Story of Success*. New York: Little, Brown and Company.

Griffiths, Mark D. 1998. "Internet Addiction: Does It Really Exist?" In *Psychology and the Internet: Intrapersonal, Interpersonal and Transpersonal Implications*, edited by J. Gackenbach, 61–75. New York: Academic Press.

Hamdy, Sherine, and Coleman Nye. (Art by Sarula Bao and Caroline Brewer). 2017. *Lissa: A Story about Medical Promise, Friendship, and Revolution.* Toronto: University of Toronto Press.

Irving, Andrew. 2017. *The Art of Life and Death: Radical Aesthetics and Ethnographic Practice.* Chicago: University of Chicago Press.

Jackson, Michael. 1986. *Barawa and the Way Birds Fly in the Sky.* Washington, DC: Smithsonian Institution Press.

Jackson, Michael. 2004. *In Sierra Leone.* Durham, NC: Duke University Press. https://doi.org/10.1215/9780822385561.

Keen, Andres. 2012. *Digital Vertigo: How Today's Online Social Revolution Is Dividing, Diminishing, and Disorienting Us.* New York: St. Martin's Press.

Narayan, Kirin. 1989. *Storytellers, Saints, and Scoundrels.* Philadelphia: University of Pennsylvania Press. https://doi.org/10.9783/9780812205831.

Narayan, Kirin. 1994. *Love, Stars, and All That.* New York: Atria.

O'Brien, Tim. 1990. *The Things They Carried.* New York: Houghton Mifflin.

Rettberg, Jill Walker. 2014. *Blogging.* 2nd ed. Cambridge, UK: Polity Press.

Rosaldo, Renato. 2014. *The Day of Shelly's Death.* Durham, NC: Duke University Press.

Rouch, Jean. 1955. *Les maîtres fous.* Paris: Films de la Pleiade.

Stoller, Paul. 1992. *The Cinematic Griot: The Ethnography of Jean Rouch.* Chicago: University of Chicago Press.

Stoller, Paul. 1999. *Jaguar: A Story of Africans in America.* Chicago: University of Chicago Press.

Stoller, Paul. 2005. *Gallery Bundu: A Story About an African Past.* Chicago: University of Chicago Press.

Stoller, Paul. 2014. *Yaya's Story: The Quest for Well-Being in the World.* Chicago: University of Chicago Press. https://doi.org/10.7208/chicago/9780226178967.001.0001.

Stoller, Paul. "The Bureau of Memories: Archives and Ephemera." Visual and New Media Review, *Cultural Anthropology* website, March 20, 2015. https://culanth.org/fieldsights/647-the-bureau-of-memories-archives-and-ephemera.

Stoller, Paul. 2015. *Cultural Anthropology Online.* Fieldsites. "The Bureau of Memories: Archives and Ephemera." Visual and New Media Review, Cultural Anthropology website, March 20, 2015. https://culanth.org/fieldsights/647-the-bureau-of-memories-archives-and-ephemera.

Stoller, Paul. 2016. *The Sorcerer's Burden: The Ethnographic Saga of a Global Family.* New York: Palgrave Macmillan. https://doi.org/10.1007/978-3-319-31805-9.

Taylor, Mark. 2014. "Speed Kills: Fast Is Never Fast Enough." *Chronicle of Higher Education,* October 20, 2014.

Ulysse, Gina. 2015. *Why Haiti Needs New Narratives: A Post-Quake Chronicle.* Middletown, CT: Wesleyan University Press.

Waterston, Alisse. 2017. "Getting Credit." *Anthropology News,* May 1, 2017. Washington, DC: American Anthropological Association.

Westera, Wim. 2013. *The Digital Turn: How the Internet Transforms Our Existence.* New York: Authorhouse.

INDEX

9 781487 594923